A CHURCH REVIVAL

A CHURCH

REVIVAL

C. E. MATTHEWS, 1887–

Charles Evert

BROADMAN PRESS · NASHVILLE, TENNESSEE

Printed in the United States of America
100.S54R.R.D.

ABOUT THE AUTHOR

DR. CHARLES E. MATTHEWS was born on a farm in Gasconade County, Missouri, March 23, 1887. His father died when the son was eleven months of age, leaving a wife and three children. The boyhood life of Dr. Matthews was one of struggle and hardship due to poor health and loss of his mother when he was sixteen.

His training was for the business world. He was an employee of Swift and Company for eleven and a half years in Fort Worth, Texas. He was married to Nana Mae Smith of Fort Worth, Texas, in 1910. They have two children living and two grandchildren.

Dr. Matthews was converted at the age of twenty-seven and was called to the ministry at the age of thirty-two. He received training at Southwestern Baptist Theological Seminary, Fort Worth. He was pastor of the Baptist Church in Birdville, Texas, one year. In 1922 he was called as pastor of Travis Avenue Baptist Church, Fort Worth, Texas, where he served for twenty-three and a half years. When he resigned to become superintendent of evangelism for the Baptist General Convention of Texas, this church had grown to be one of the great churches of Texas.

Since January 1, 1947, Dr. Matthews has been secretary of evangelism for the Home Mission Board.

Dr. Matthews is the author of several books, including *Life's Supreme Decision, The Southern Baptist Program of Evangelism,* and *Every Christian's Job.*

Through the leadership of the Department of Evangelism, in full co-operation with all other agencies of the Southern Baptist Convention, the number of baptisms in Southern Baptist churches has increased 50.9 per cent in recent years.

CONTENTS

1

The Origin of the Church

"And Jesus answered and said unto him, Blessed art thou, Simon Barjona: for flesh and blood hath not revealed it unto thee, but my Father which is in heaven. And I say also unto thee, That thou art Peter, and upon this rock I will build my church; and the gates of hell shall not prevail against it" (Matt. 16: 17-18).

The subject of this book, A CHURCH REVIVAL, expresses the purpose for which it is intended. Much is being written today on the subject of evangelism, but little is said about a church revival. There is a reason for this. The tendency of the times is to disregard the church and to emphasize "movements" as far as evangelism is concerned.

I. THE SOURCE OF INFORMATION ABOUT THE CHURCH

There is only one reliable source of information about the church of the Lord Jesus Christ. That source is the Bible. It may be asked, Then why are there in the world so many different kinds of organizations which call themselves churches? If the founders of all of the existing religious groups obtained their information from one book as to what a New Testament church is, why then is there such a variety of denominations with such contrasts in their beliefs and practices? The explanation is this: The Bible is not an ordinary book. Its author is God. Men wrote the Bible as they were moved by the Holy Spirit. This is a Baptist distinctive: "We believe that the Holy Bible was

1

written by men divinely inspired, and is a perfect
treasure of heavenly instruction: that it has God for
its author, salvation for its end, and truth without any
mixture of error, for its matter; that it reveals the
principles by which God will judge us; and therefore
is, and shall remain to the end of the world, the true
center of Christian union, and the supreme standard
by which all human conduct, creeds, and opinions
should be tried."

God is infinite and man is finite. It is not possible for
a finite being to understand all that is disclosed by an
infinite being. For that reason alone there is bound to
be a variety of opinions among sincere men as to what
the Bible teaches about the church as well as what
it teaches about other matters. Many denominations
came into existence because of the views of their
founders. Space does not permit mentioning and
discussing the founders of various denominational
groups. It is not even possible to tell what all the various Baptist groups believe concerning the origin of
the church. Therefore, this discussion is confined to
the view of the church held by Southern Baptists.

II. JESUS FOUNDED HIS CHURCH

For one who believes the New Testament to be the
inspired Word of God, the question, Who founded
the New Testament Church? is answered with one
simple concise statement, found in Matthew 16: 18:
"And I say also unto thee, That thou art Peter, and
upon this rock I will build my church; and the gates
of hell shall not prevail against it."

Dr. E. C. Routh in his splendid book *Who Are
They?* says: "Our people have not always been called
'Baptists,' but in their beliefs and polity they are sub-
stantially identical with New Testament churches. Un-

like many other denominations, Baptists did not begin within the last few centuries with some human personality. The real succession which Baptists cherish is not historical or the persistence of some name, but a spiritual identity with groups of believers, in apostolic days and on through the centuries, who accepted and practiced what the New Testament teaches. Baptist churches would not be affected if every man-made creed were wiped out. With us the Bible is our sole and sufficient rule of faith and practice.

"Within a century or two after the resurrection and ascension of our Lord, the early churches were disturbed by 'unruly and vain talkers and deceivers.' In the epistles of the New Testament are references to subverters of those days who taught salvation by law rather than by grace, or denied the deity and resurrection of Christ, and engaged in endless controversies which settled nothing and led nowhere. Soon, there emerged the heresies of baptismal regeneration, infant baptism, the dominance of certain bishops over other bishops, the control of religion by the State, and the persecution of dissenters. But all the way along, even through the Dark Ages, there were groups of believers who, like their Lord, endured the cross, despising the shame. They were called various names, but they were true to the only Name, the Name above every name, by which sinners may be saved and saints sustained and strengthened. Whatever their name, they believed in soul-liberty, salvation by grace, a regenerated church membership, the priesthood of believers, believer's baptism, and separation of Church and State. They blazed a trail ofttimes marked by the blood of their devotion to the Word of God." [1]

---

[1] E. C. Routh, *Who Are They?* (Shawnee: O.B.U. Press, 1952), pp. 66–67.

Dr. Routh has stated the view of Baptists concerning the New Testament church. We would add to his statement "believer's baptism" the word "immersion." There is not a line or a syllable in the New Testament which would indicate directly or indirectly that believers were not immersed or buried in water when they were baptized. With all of the understanding we possess, we can say that a Southern Baptist church fits in every way the description of the church which Jesus founded. It is our most sacred duty to God and to all humanity to keep in line with the pattern of the church Christ founded.

1. When Did Jesus Found His Church?

The question, When did Jesus found his church? may seem irrelevant to some, but it has deep bearing and significance as to certain heresies that always crop out where the least semblance of uncertainty prevails. Baptists are emphatic as to when the church was founded by our Lord.

It is a fact that Christians as a rule, and preachers in particular, have largely formed their theological viewpoints and their religious tendencies from those who taught them. For instance, most Lutherans are of that sect because they were taught by Lutheran teachers. The same can be said of Catholics, Methodists, Presbyterians, and Baptists. There are, of course, some exceptions. The Holy Spirit, if given the right of way in the individual's search for truth, will make some changes in his convictions.

The author's textbook on theology in the seminary was by Dr. E. Y. Mullins, taught by Dr. W. T. Conner. The application of the contents of Bible truth as touching the church and evangelism was by Dr. L. R. Scarborough. These teachers were Southern Baptists.

They were fundamental in doctrinal belief and its application to life. They were strict denominational-ists with a genuine Christian attitude toward all believers of other faiths. They all held closely to the Baptist distinctives which have made Southern Baptists a "peculiar people." The author believes that these principles have been responsible more than any other one factor for the unprecedented growth of Southern Baptists and their tremendous influence throughout the world where they have been taught.

Jesus founded his church when he was here in the flesh before his death on the cross. There are six definite proofs of this.

(1) *There were baptized believers while Jesus was here in the flesh.*—"Wherefore of these men which have companied with us all the time that the Lord Jesus went in and out among us, beginning from the baptism of John, unto that same day that he was taken up from us, must one be ordained to be a witness with us of his resurrection" (Acts 1: 21-22).

(2) *The disciples who were with Jesus while he was in the flesh had an organization.*—Judas was its treasurer.

(3) *Those who were disciples with Jesus in the flesh had both church ordinances.*—These are baptism and the Lord's Supper.

(4) *Christ told his disciples to take their problems of discipline to the church.*—"Moreover if thy brother shall trespass against thee, go and tell him his fault between thee and him alone: if he shall hear thee, thou hast gained thy brother. But if he will not hear thee, then take with thee one or two more, that in the mouth of two or three witnesses every word may be established. And if he shall neglect to hear them, tell it unto the church: but if he neglect to hear the church,

let him be unto thee as an heathen man and a publi-
can" (Matt. 18: 15-17). How could this be done if no
church existed?

(5) *The converts at Pentecost were added to the
church.*—How could this have been done if there had
been no church?

(6) *The Great Commission was given to the church.*
—It was given near the time of Christ's departure from
the earth back to the Father. This is one reason, and
the principal reason, why baptism is considered to be
a church ordinance. Jesus commanded his church to
baptize disciples. That the Great Commission was
given to the church is the reason for considering missions a church obligation. *If missions is a church obligation, evangelism is, too.* If the Great Commission
was given to the church, then there must have been a
church in existence. In what other manner can anyone
interpret these words of our Lord, "Go ye therefore,
and teach all nations, baptizing them in the name of
the Father, and of the Son, and of the Holy Ghost:
teaching them to observe all things whatsoever I have
commanded you: and, lo, I am with you alway, even
unto the end of the world"? (Matt. 28: 19-20).

2. Why the Importance Attached to the Time Christ Founded His Church?

The fact of whether or not Christ founded his
church while here in the flesh is of tremendous importance. Here are some of the reasons.

(1) *The Great Commission.*—If there were no
church at the time he gave his Great Commission,
then it was given to individual believers; and when
they died, the commission was invalid. Individuals
do not perpetuate; churches do.

(2) *The ordinances.*—If baptism and the Lord's

Supper were observed when there was no church, then these ordinances do not belong to the church.

(3) *The authority of the church.*—If there were no church before Pentecost (as many professed believers claim), all that was done by the followers of Christ before that time was not under the authority of the church. This then destroys the significance it has in the New Testament. Dr. W. R. White in his book *Baptist Distinctives* says: "Baptists have given the word 'church' the dominant significance it has in the New Testament. *Ecclesia* had a very fixed meaning in the Greek mind. It meant a local assembly. It was called out and together for a specific purpose and had distinct functions. It was independent and autonomous. Of the 117 times it appears in the New Testament, at least 92 times it is used in this primary sense. The other uses are not inconsistent with this idea.

"There is no actual, functioning universal church, whether invisible or visible, in existence today. Nowhere is such an idea taught in the New Testament. All redeemed men and women of all ages, whether on earth or in heaven, belong to the family of God (Eph. 3: 15). Every born-again believer is in the kingdom of God (John 3: 15). But only baptized believers in the fellowship of a local body, having the New Testament as its law and only law, belong to a functioning New Testament church.

"It is true that all Christians are numbered with that accumulating body of Christ which is unassembled—that congregation of Christ which is not yet congregated. After the resurrection it will assemble and will then become a functioning church of Christ. All Christians are members in prospect of that coming church (Heb. 12: 23; Rev. 19: 6-8). This seeming contradiction is a paradox. There is a sense in which

Baptists both exclude and include others as related to
the church of Christ. Others are in the forming but
not the functioning body." [1]

This remarkably plain and significant statement by
Dr. White is exactly what the author believes concerning the New Testament church and the functioning
purpose Christ had for it in this world. Almost everything that can be done in soul-winning through the
church can possibly be done outside the church, for
the simple reason that the Holy Spirit dwells in every
redeemed soul. But it was Christ's plan for his church
to carry on the work that he began in his early ministry. The church is the unit or assembly over which a
shepherd is appointed by the Holy Spirit as an over-
seer. "Take heed therefore unto yourselves, and to all
the flock, over the which the Holy Ghost hath made
you overseers, to feed the church of God, which he
hath purchased with his own blood" (Acts 20: 28).
God's sheep can wander without a shepherd or they
can be led, supervised, and directed by a shepherd.
That is why Baptists believe in church-centered evangelism.

Outline for Teacher

I. THE SOURCE OF INFORMATION ABOUT THE CHURCH

II. JESUS FOUNDED HIS CHURCH

    1. When Did Jesus Found His Church?

        (1) There were baptized believers while Jesus
            was here in the flesh.

        (2) The disciples who were with Jesus while he
            was in the flesh had an organization.

---

[1] W. R. White, *Baptist Distinctives* (Nashville: The Sunday School
Board of the Southern Baptist Convention, 1946), pp. 53–54.

(3) Those who were disciples with Jesus in the flesh had both church ordinances.
(4) Christ told his disciples to take their problems of discipline to the church.
(5) The converts at Pentecost were added to the church.
(6) The Great Commission was given to the church.

2. Why the Importance Attached to the Time Christ Founded His Church?
   (1) The Great Commission
   (2) The ordinances
   (3) The authority of the church

Suggestions to Teacher

1. Assign names of prospects for the church to class members each night for visitation.
2. Have a report on visitation each night.

2

Christ's Purpose for His Church

NEXT in order for a church revival is an understanding of the purpose Christ has for his church. This purpose is set out in the Great Commission.

I. THE BIBLE A BOOK OF MANY PURPOSES

The Bible is a book of many purposes. Some study it for its value in the field of law. Gladstone once said that all moral and civil law is based upon the teachings of the Bible. Some study the Bible for its historical value. It contains the only complete history of the human race, beginning with Adam. In it is the record of past events of mankind and prophecies foretelling future events concerning the human race. Others study the Bible for its literary value. Undoubtedly, it is the gem of all literature, both prose and poetry. Some study it for its value in character building. In this it certainly excels all other books.

Evangelists see in the Bible the history of a conflict, a warfare indescribable in its fury and destructiveness. That warfare is carried on between God and his righteous forces against Satan and his forces of evil. The mention of its beginning is found in Isaiah: "Hell from beneath is moved for thee to meet thee at thy coming: it stirreth up the dead for thee, even all the chief ones of the earth; it hath raised up from their thrones all the kings of the nations. All they shall speak and say unto thee, Art thou also become weak as we? art thou become like unto us? Thy pomp is brought down to the grave, and the noise of thy viols: the worm is spread under thee, and the worms cover thee. How art thou fallen from heaven, O Lucifer, son of the morning! how art thou cut down to the ground, which didst weaken the nations! For thou hast said in thine heart, I will ascend into heaven, I will exalt my throne above the stars of God: I will sit also upon the mount of the congregation, in the sides of the north: I will ascend above the heights of the clouds; I will be like the most High. Yet thou shalt be brought down to hell, to the sides of the pit. They that see thee shall narrowly look upon thee, and consider thee, saying, Is this the man that made the earth to tremble, that did shake kingdoms; that made the world as a wilderness, and destroyed the cities thereof; that opened not the house of his prisoners?" (Isa. 14: 9-17).

"And there was war in heaven: Michael and his angels fought against the dragon; and the dragon fought and his angels, and prevailed not; neither was their place found any more in heaven. And the great dragon was cast out, that old serpent, called the Devil, and Satan, which deceiveth the whole world: he was cast out into the earth, and his angels were cast out with him. And I heard a loud voice saying in heaven, Now is come salvation, and strength, and the kingdom of our God, and the power of his Christ: for the accuser of our brethren is cast down, which accused them before our God day and night" (Rev. 12: 7-10).

"And he said unto them, I beheld Satan as lightning fall from heaven" (Luke 10: 18).

All humanity is on one side or the other in this horrible conflict. There is no neutral ground. "No servant can serve two masters: for either he will hate the one, and love the other; or else he will hold to the one, and despise the other. Ye cannot serve God and mammon" (Luke 16: 13). "He that is not with me is against me: and he that gathereth not with me scattereth" (Luke 11: 23). Christians shall suffer persecution (2 Tim. 3: 12).

The apostle Paul so clearly understood this warfare and was so involved in it that he uses the terminology of a physical warfare in his writings. He pictures the Christian as a soldier of the cross enlisted in the great army of God. In Ephesians 6 he uses military terms in describing the uniform of a Spirit-filled believer. "Finally, my brethren, be strong in the Lord, and in the power of his might. Put on the whole armour of God, that ye may be able to stand against the wiles of the devil. For we wrestle not against flesh and blood, but against principalities, against powers, against the rulers of the darkness of this world, against spiritual wickedness in high places. Wherefore take unto you the whole armour of God, that ye may be able to withstand in the evil day, and having done all, to stand. Stand therefore, having your loins girt about with truth, and having on the breastplate of righteousness; and your feet shod with the preparation of the gospel of peace; above all, taking the shield of faith, wherewith ye shall be able to quench all the fiery darts of the wicked. And take the helmet of salvation, and the sword of the Spirit, which is the word of God" (Eph. 6: 10-17). With Paul and other preachers of the New Testament era, the Bible is a spiritual weapon, "the sword of the Spirit, which is the word of God" (Eph. 6: 17).

II. THE CHURCH IN THE GREAT CONFLICT

Throughout the Bible there is a raging conflict between the forces of light and the powers of darkness. In the beginning of the first book Satan engages in his vicious and subtle attack in the garden of Eden. In the last book of the Bible he suffers his last and final defeat at the hands of a righteous God. "And when the thousand years are expired, Satan shall be loosed out of his prison, and shall go out to deceive the nations which are in the four quarters of the earth, Gog and Magog, to gather them together to battle: the number of whom is as the sand of the sea. And they went up on the breadth of the earth, and compassed the camp of the saints about, and the beloved city: and fire came down from God out of heaven and devoured them. and the devil that deceived them was cast into the lake of fire and brimstone, where the beast and the false prophet are, and shall be tormented day and night for ever and ever" (Rev. 20: 7-10).

In this long and seemingly endless conflict, time is divided into two periods. The history of these periods recorded in the Bible shows how God is working out his purposes in this terrible conflict unto death against his formidable foe. Well are Christians acquainted with the age of law which began with Moses and ended at the cross. Then began the age of grace, in which period we are now living. Christ is the fulfillment of the law. In the march of time we see five things.

1. *The Coming of Jesus to Establish His Church*

God took a long time to prepare this world for the birth of his Son. Jesus could have been born when Adam sinned or at any other period chosen of God, for his birth and his death were known to the Father before the foundation of the world. It was not until the fulness of time, when all preparation was consummated and the world was ready, that Jesus appeared in the flesh. "Now I say, That the heir, as long as he is a child, differeth nothing from a servant, though he be lord of all; but is under tutors and governors until the time appointed of the father. Even so we, when we were children, were in bondage under the elements of the world: but when the fulness of the time was come, God sent forth his Son, made of a woman, made under the law, to redeem them that were under the law, that we might receive the adoption of sons" (Gal. 4: 1-5).

2. *The Church Established and Victory for It Assured*

When Christ revealed himself as the Messiah, he established his church and gave to it his guarantee of victory. No other institution, society, or form of government, has this guarantee of victory. Such an indisputable guarantee is only for his church. "And I say also unto thee, That thou art Peter, and upon this rock I will build my church; and the gates of hell shall not prevail against it" (Matt. 16: 18). What inspiration and encouragement this should be to Christians everywhere in these testing times! Constantly on every hand we hear the question, Has the church failed? Some churches are weak and many of them have died or disbanded. But where one dies, another springs up. In some of the older countries where churches once flourished, their candlesticks are now removed, but in their stead other churches have sprung up in new points of the world and they thrive with greater spiritual zeal and power than ever. This is typical of the churches in the United States. The pilgrim fathers left a world of spiritual destitution. They founded a new civilization here where there are more churches than ever existed in any two nations in history.

3. Christ and His Church Interrelated

The relationship of Christ and his church is probably the most peculiar relationship that exists in heaven or in earth. Figures of speech are used to explain the relationship of Christ and his church. In one instance the church is a house of prayer. "And said unto them, It is written, My house shall be called the house of prayer; but ye have made it a den of thieves" (Matt. 21: 13). In another instance it is the house of God and the pillar and ground of the truth. "But if I tarry long, that thou mayest know how thou oughtest to behave thyself in the house of God, which is the church of the living God, the pillar and ground of the truth" (1 Tim. 3: 15). In another, it is a body. "Now ye are the body of Christ, and members in particular. And God hath set some in the church, first apostles, secondarily prophets, thirdly teachers, after that miracles, then gifts of healings, helps, governments, diversities of tongues" (1 Cor. 12: 27-28).

In another place Christ is the head and the church his body. "And hath put all things under his feet, and gave him to be the head over all things to the church, which is his body, the fulness of him that filleth all in all" (Eph. 1: 22-23). The best illustration of this relationship, if one could be called the best, is that which calls Christ the groom and the church his bride. "For I am jealous over you with godly jealousy: for I have espoused you to one husband, that I may present you as a chaste virgin to Christ" (2 Cor. 11: 2). "And there came unto me one of the seven angels which had the seven vials full of the seven last plagues, and talked

with me, saying, Come hither, I will shew thee the
bride, the Lamb's wife" (Rev. 21: 9). No relationship
could be closer than that of husband and wife, for
they are no longer two but one.

The fact of this relationship is brought vividly to
our attention in Christ's statement to Saul of Tarsus
at the time of the latter's conversion. Until that time,
Saul had never seen Jesus. Saul hated the Christian
movement. His anger and his hatred were so intensified that he not only persecuted the church, but was
a party to the execution of its leaders. While on the
road to Damascus to further this mad mission of de-
struction, he heard a voice from heaven, saying, "Why
persecutest thou me?" "At midday, O king, I saw in
the way a light from heaven, above the brightness of
the sun, shining round about me and them which
journeyed with me. And when we were all fallen to
the earth, I heard a voice speaking unto me, and saying
in the Hebrew tongue, Saul, Saul, why persecutest
thou me? it is hard for thee to kick against the pricks.
And I said, Who art thou, Lord? And he said, I am
Jesus whom thou persecutest" (Acts 26: 13-15). Here
Jesus clearly declares that he and the church are one,
just as husband and wife are bone of each other's bone
and flesh of each other's flesh.

4. *The Meaning of the Relationship of Christ and His
Church*

(1) *The strength of Christ in this world is in his
churches.*—Close the doors of all of the churches in
America and the American way of life would not last
six months. Cherished freedoms would be lost. Com-
munism or some other form of despotism would soon
hold sway.

(2) *The mission of Christ while here in the flesh*

is the mission of his churches.—It could not be otherwise. They are one and the same, organically and in purpose.

5. THE PURPOSE OF CHRIST AND HIS CHURCH

Jesus came to seek and to save that which was lost (Luke 19: 10). That is exactly the meaning of the Great Commission as given to his church before he departed to be with the Father. The commission has three definite aspects.

(1) *To make disciples, leading people from darkness to light and from the power of Satan unto God.*— That is what is called soul-winning. But that is only the beginning of evangelism in the true sense as engaged in by Jesus in his earthly ministry and as meant in the Great Commission. For a sinner to accept Christ as Saviour is a glorious thing, but to stop there is a tragedy. It makes no difference how the decision is brought about or where it happens; when one experiences regeneration, he is a child of God and bound for heaven. This can be done without reference to a church.

(2) *To baptize them in the name of the Father, and of the Son, and of the Holy Ghost is the first act of obedience on the part of a believer in Christ.*—That is where the church comes in, for baptism is a church ordinance. "Now I praise you, brethren, that ye remember me in all things, and keep the ordinances, as I delivered them to you" (1 Cor. 11: 2).

(3) *"Teaching them to observe all things whatsoever I have commanded you" is the third aspect of Christ-centered and church-centered evangelism.*— To "observe," as stated here, means more than to look or to take notice. It means to learn, to train, to do, to perform, and to participate.

One can be saved and leave the church completely out of his life as to his activities. That is tragically true of multitudes of professed believers today. It is impossible to carry out the Great Commission in full, separate from the church. The primal work of Southern Baptists throughout the history of their Convention has been their effort to carry out Christ's commission in full by centering all of their efforts through their churches. This is true in stewardship. To do otherwise would destroy the Cooperative Program. The unified church budget has been the salvation of all Southern Baptist work from the financial standpoint. If the members of our churches were to break with the scriptural method of paying their tithes and offerings through the church treasury and submitting the distribution of funds to the plan of the church, the organized work of the denomination would fall apart in a short time. If church members sent their tithes and offerings as they chose to this or to that person or cause instead of channeling them through the church, our educational institutions, our benevolent work, and our mission program would completely fail.

What is true of stewardship and missions is also true of evangelism. Jesus made it that way. If we desert our churches in revival effort because it is difficult and not as attractive as some other method or for any other reason, our churches will lose their spiritual fervor and zeal and grow cold and powerless. Church-centered evangelism is not an easy method, and it appears slow at times; but it is Christ's way and it is the victorious way.

III. CHRIST'S ADVERSARY IS THE CHURCH'S ADVERSARY

That Satan hates Christ goes without saying. Satan tried to destroy Jesus when he was a babe. Again and again he plotted to kill Jesus through the efforts of wicked men. Satan in his diabolical schemes even tempted our Saviour forty days to commit sin and thus destroy the purpose of his mission in the world. In the same manner Satan hates the church. He hates it with a passion almost equal to that of Christ's love for his church. Satan succeeded in blinding Israel and led its people to crucify their long promised Messiah. "The God of Abraham, and of Isaac, and of Jacob, the God of our fathers, hath glorified his Son Jesus; whom ye delivered up, and denied him in the presence of Pilate, when he was determined to let him go. But ye denied the Holy One and the Just, and desired a murderer to be granted unto you; and killed the Prince of life, whom God hath raised from the dead; whereof we are witnesses" (Acts 3: 13-15). In like manner the devil has blinded many church members today to be disloyal to their churches.

Take a close look at what Satan did to the seven churches as recorded in the second and third chapters of Revelation. He caused the church at Ephesus to leave her first love. At Smyrna he placed blasphemers in the church, people who belonged to Satan's synagogue. He went still farther and cast some of the faithful members into prison. "Fear none of those things which thou shalt suffer: behold, the devil shall cast some of you into prison, that ye may be tried; and ye shall have tribulation ten days: be thou faithful unto death, and I will give thee a crown of life" (Rev. 2: 10).

At Pergamos it is almost unbelievable that we read, "And to the angel of the church in Pergamos write: These things saith he which hath the sharp sword with two edges; I know thy works, and where thou dwellest, even where Satan's seat is: and thou holdest fast my name, and hast not denied my faith, even in those days

wherein Antipas was my faithful martyr, who was
slain among you, where Satan dwelleth" (Rev. 2:
12-13). Think of it; Satan has his headquarters in a
church.

At Thyatira, a genuine Jezebel was in the church
calling herself a prophetess and leading members of
the church into idolatry and fornication. The church
in Sardis had been poisoned with the opiate of the
sin of indifference and unconcern and was spiritually
dead. In 1953 more than five thousand Southern Baptist churches reported no baptisms. What would Jesus
say of a church that reported not one baptism in an
entire year?

The church in Philadelphia, the best of the lot, had
Satan's people out of his synagogue in it. "Behold, I
will make them of the synagogue of Satan, which say
they are Jews, and are not, but do lie; behold, I will
make them to come and worship before thy feet, and
to know that I have loved thee" (Rev. 3: 9).

The last of the seven, the church of the Laodiceans,
a materially rich church but shamefully destitute and
naked of spiritual power, was lukewarm to the extent
that it nauseated Christ. Could Satan do anything
more to cripple and to destroy the churches of Christ
than he did to these seven churches? He is carrying
on today with an aggressiveness beyond anything we
read about in the Bible.

The author, while filling a speaking engagement in
a northern city, heard a report on evangelism. The
report included 116 Baptist churches with an average
of four baptisms per church for the preceding year.
The next day he was present in an evangelistic service
where some two thousand young people were present.
The speaker on the occasion brought a good message.
He stated that the movement which he represented

had "witnessed the sweeping of thousands into the kingdom of God." The speaker was supposed to be a Baptist. The next day one of the officials of the movement (which was ecumenical in its aspect) said to the author: "I appreciated seeing you in our services yesterday. What do you think of our movement?" I answered, "It is doomed to failure." "Why do you say that?" he asked. I replied, "Because it by-passes the churches." He said, "The churches up here are dead." "You had better resurrect them," I replied, "if your work is to be permanent." Again it may be asked, What more could Satan do to a church than he did to the seven churches of Revelation? Did Christ give them up? Did he turn his back on them and forsake them? No, he commanded them to repent! He wanted them to be revived.

That is what he is crying out to his churches throughout the world today: Repent and be revived! Every church needs a revival. A revival is as essential to the Christian's heart as rain is to the ground. A genuine heaven-sent revival of the Christian religion is the supreme need of this hour. A hunger for God should be in the heart of every child of God as Christians face their adversary who seems to be parading up and down this earth as a bloodthirsty, roaring lion, seeking whom he may devour. God is ready to send that needed revival when the churches are ready to receive it.

Revive us again;
Fill each heart with Thy love;
May each soul be rekindled with fire from above.
Hallelujah! Thine the glory,
Hallelujah! amen;
Hallelujah! Thine the glory,
Revive us again.

Outline for Teacher

I. THE BIBLE A BOOK OF MANY PURPOSES

II. THE CHURCH IN THE GREAT CONFLICT

1. The Coming of Jesus to Establish His Church

2. The Church Established and Victory for It Assured

3. Christ and His Church Interrelated

4. The Meaning of the Relationship of Christ and His Church

   (1) The strength of Christ in this world is in his churches.

   (2) The mission of Christ while here in the flesh is the mission of his churches.

5. The Purpose of Christ and His Church

   (1) To make disciples, leading people from darkness to light and from the power of Satan unto God.

   (2) To baptize them in the name of the Father, and of the Son, and of the Holy Ghost is the first act of obedience on the part of a believer in Christ.

   (3) "Teaching them to observe all things whatsoever I have commanded you" is the third aspect of Christ-centered evangelism.

III. CHRIST'S ADVERSARY IS THE CHURCH'S ADVERSARY

Suggestions to Teacher

1. Continue to assign names of prospects each night.

2. Have a report on visitation each night.

3

Planning a Church Revival

IT IS AT the point of planning a church revival that a church succeeds or fails in soul-winning. A church seldom does more than it plans for in any endeavor. If an individual makes no plans for the future, his life becomes a hit or miss proposition. In the same way, a church that does not plan to win souls will not win many.

The basis for planning anything in life stems from a concept of its importance. If a thing is of no importance, then no plans need be made for it. If it is of vital importance, then it is foolish not to plan for it. Probably the most significant act of God in this respect was his creation of Adam and Eve. The Bible makes clear that man is before angels in God's divine purpose for the consummation of his kingdom. "But to which of the angels said he at any time, Sit on my right hand, until I make thine enemies thy footstool? Are they not all ministering spirits, sent forth to minister for them who shall be heirs of salvation?" (Heb. 1: 13-14).

It is a sure thing that man is of more value than material things. "For what shall it profit a man, if he shall gain the whole world, and lose his own soul? Or what shall a man give in exchange for his soul?" (Mark 8: 36-37).

Plans for man's spiritual needs and plans for his redemption were made in the heart of God from the beginning. The most comforting promise recorded in the Bible is John 14: 1-6: "Let not your heart be troubled:

ye believe in God, believe also in me. In my Father's house are many mansions: if it were not so, I would have told you. I go to prepare a place for you. And if I go and prepare a place for you, I will come again, and receive you unto myself; that where I am, there ye may be also. And whither I go ye know, and the way ye know. Thomas saith unto him, Lord, we know not whither thou goest; and how can we know the way? Jesus saith unto him, I am the way, the truth, and the life: no man cometh unto the Father, but by me." Here Jesus tells his disciples that his plans are already consummated for them in heaven.

I. THE RESULTS OF PLANNING EVANGELISM THROUGH THE CHURCHES

The term "evangelism" instead of "soul-winning" is used here because evangelism covers the Great Commission of Christ to his church, while soul-winning covers only the first aspect of the commission, "make disciples."

Southern Baptists have always been evangelistic in spirit and in purpose. Each organization in the church has its place in the plans of the church for evangelizing the masses. The Sunday school has ever been the most active of church organizations in this respect. The Training Union and the Woman's Missionary Union have made and are making their contribution to the Southern Baptist program of evangelism. The Brotherhood, too, stands ready to do anything the pastor and the church may suggest toward helping to evangelize the community.

Some years ago many of our churches had quit trying to have revivals, and baptisms were at the alarming rate of 1 to every 27 church members in the Southern Baptist Convention. The Convention in session at Miami, Florida, in 1946, voted to appoint a committee composed of representatives from all of the states to draft a program of evangelism for consideration by the Convention in its next session in St. Louis, Missouri, in 1947. The committee presented a program as instructed. This draft is outlined in the book *The Southern Baptist Program of Evangelism* by Matthews, which may be secured from any Baptist Book Store. The results in baptisms in Southern Baptist churches for the ensuing years have indeed been gratifying.

The average gain in baptisms per year for the seven years (1947-1953) of the adopted program over the seven years previous to its adoption was 114,757.

The total gain in baptisms in the seven years of the adopted program over the seven years previous to its adoption was 803,295.

The department of evangelism of the Home Mission Board acts as a co-ordinating agency in this program of promoting evangelism. The work of evangelism is carried on by the churches through their existing church organizations.

II. THE EVANGELISM CHURCH COUNCIL ESSENTIAL IN PLANNING CHURCH REVIVALS

In the Southern Baptist program of evangelism, recommended by the Southern Baptist Convention to the churches, a planning committee called the evangelism church council, or the pastor's cabinet, is suggested for every church. Thousands of churches in the Convention have this council or cabinet. Let us consider in detail what this council is and does in evangelism.

1. *Personnel*

The council is composed of the pastor (in all instances the chairman), the Sunday school superintendent, the Training Union director, the Woman's Missionary Union president, the president of the Brotherhood, the council secretary, and the educational director, where there is one, and any other church officer desired.

The evangelism church council is composed of the same people who serve with the pastor on the church council, the co-ordinating group for all church activities.

2. When Does the Evangelism Council Meet?

The evangelism church council should meet annually early in October. There should be as many other meetings as the chairman may deem necessary.

3. Duties of the Council

The duties of the evangelism church council are as follows:

(1) *It is the church planning committee for evangelism.*—Its plans for the program of evangelism to be presented to the church for adoption are suggested here.

a. Two revivals each year.—One of these should be in co-operation with the association-wide simultaneous crusade. In order for the dates to be set wisely, the following information should be in possession of the chairman: calendar of activities of the Sunday school, W.M.U., Training Union, and Brotherhood, with all of their major events and study courses; dates of associational meetings; dates of state meetings; schedule of dates for the meeting of the Southern Baptist Convention and its assemblies at Glorieta and Ridgecrest; dates of civic or community meetings that would seriously interfere with revival meetings.

With this information in hand the committee can

plan revival meetings with the assurance of a minimum of conflict with other meetings.

The reason for meeting in October is obvious. It gives the church time to secure evangelistic help. It provides time for adequate preparation for a revival. It expresses the will and the wisdom of the pastor and leaders of the existing church organizations. If these organizations have a part in planning for the revival, they will feel that it is their revival, and will co-operate more readily.

b. A calendar of visitation.—This calendar should rotate by agencies week by week the year around.

c. A time for the church members to study soul-winning.—Courses are provided for this purpose in the Graded Training Union Study Course.

(2) *It is to institute methods for finding prospects for evangelistic efforts.*

a. By taking an annual religious census.

b. By locating prospects that move into the community between census takings.—This may be done through the Woman's Missionary Union circles.

c. By planning for visitors' cards to be passed out during church services.—This is a valuable source of prospects.

d. Through information from other sources.—The Chamber of Commerce, public utilities, or business firms may give this information.

(3) *It is to keep accurate records of prospects.*

a. Their names and addresses.

b. A list of live prospects.—This may be done by eliminating names of all that join the church from week to week; by eliminating names of those who, it is discovered, are not prospects; and by dropping names of those who have moved out of the community or died.

(4) *It is to see that a class for new church members is conducted through the Training Union.*—The book suggested is *Your Life and Your Church* by James L. Sullivan.

4. *Advantages of Having the Evangelism Council*

A functioning evangelism council is practical for any church, regardless of size or location. Some of the smaller churches may have fewer organizations than the larger churches, but the council is just as essential in a small church as in a large church. The council may discuss, for example, the merits of two revivals each year, coming at the time when they would be most practical for reaching the lost. One church revival a year is not enough. Churches which have only one revival of eight days' duration usually have a small number of baptisms compared with the church membership.

III. THE SIMULTANEOUS EVANGELISTIC CRUSADE

The simultaneous evangelistic crusade has many advantages over other methods in evangelism.

1. *What It Is*

The simultaneous evangelistic crusade is a concerted effort of all of the churches in a given territory doing the same thing in the same way at the same time.

2. *Advantages of the Simultaneous Evangelistic Crusade*

Here are some of the advantages of the simultaneous evangelistic crusade.

It is church centered. The revivals are all conducted in the co-operating churches. It employs all of the church organizations. It strengthens every phase of local church work and makes possible conservation of results.

It will, if properly directed, command the attention of both saints and sinners.

It fixes responsibility with individuals and churches. The association-wide revival crusade enlists every church and employs an army of people.

It leaves the prospects without an excuse. There is a church in every community.

It gives every church, large or small, the same assistance and direction in leadership. It places the churches on an equal basis.

It enables any state, regardless of size, to have at least one revival in every church and unchurched community every year, something that no other method known to Southern Baptists can do.

The association-wide simultaneous crusade properly conducted is the answer to the problem of churches making an annual report of no baptisms.

It crystallizes preparation. The simultaneous crusade, if carried through, solves the problem of preparation for a revival. This is vital in any program of evangelism.

3. *It Should Be Conducted Annually*

(1) *An annual crusade produces better results.*— The question is asked, Should an association engage in a simultaneous revival each year? The answer is emphatically, "Yes. Why not?" It produces greater results in every way than any other method. Then why substitute some other less productive method for it? The excuse is an obvious one. To put on an association-wide simultaneous crusade takes work, and not everyone likes to work. It does not require much effort on the part of a pastor and church just to "jump up" the

average eight-day meeting. About all that is done to
prepare for the average single church revival is to secure an evangelist, put an advertisement in the paper,
make some announcements, and have some prayer
meetings. The community hears little about it, and
usually a large percentage of the members of the
church never know it took place until they see an article at the close of the meeting in the church bulletin.
Such an article may read: Our revival is over; now let's
settle down to work. Of course, a genuine revival can
be had in any church at any time, provided conditions
required of God for a revival are met. That is exactly
what the program of preparation for a simultaneous
evangelistic crusade does. There are associations
that have had from three to ten consecutive annual
simultaneous crusades. They become more effective and fruitful each year. The association that has
had ten consecutive simultaneous crusades had better
results in the last crusade than in any of the other nine.

(2) *A testimony.*—The Oklahoma Baptist Association, in which Oklahoma City is located, has had ten
consecutive annual simultaneous crusades. Dr. Her-
schel Hobbs, the pastor of the First Baptist Church of
Oklahoma City, gives his testimony of this method.

"There are four inclusive reasons why I believe in
the simultaneous revival program above all others.

"First, it is church centered. In the New Testament
the local church is fundamental in all Christian effort.
That which detracts from its importance should be
examined with care before allowing it to become a part
of our program. The simultaneous revival magnifies
the local church both in responsibility and results. As
such, it lends its strength to the building up of the entire denomination, magnifying the basic principles of
our faith.

"Second, it is city- or association-wide. While it magnifies the local church, it serves also to blanket a given area with the gospel of Christ. Instead of centering the efforts of the revival in one massive gathering, it brings the evangelistic effort down to the basis of community needs.

"Third, it is co-operative in its effort. Baptists do best that which they do together. Instead of each individual church becoming a lone voice crying in the wilderness, there is a unison of proclamation and appeal. The simultaneous revival enables the stronger churches to lend aid to the weaker ones. Likewise, the spirit of evangelistic zeal found in some churches serves to kindle fires of evangelism in those which are less zealous. Furthermore, the simultaneous revival program gives an excellent opportunity for racial co-operation in the great task of evangelism.

"Fourth, it is cumulative in results. No other revival program has proved as successful in enlisting converts into church membership and into subsequent growth and service. Consecutive revivals of this kind year after year give added momentum to the effort.

"The Oklahoma County Baptist Association has had a simultaneous revival for ten years without a break, the longest unbroken series anywhere. Each year it grows in power and results. In 1952 with less than 100 churches, white and Negro, participating, there were 1,969 additions, 808 for baptism. In 1953 with 100 churches involved there were 2,307 additions, 1,424 for baptism. In 1954 with 117 churches involved, there were 2,647 additions, 1,565 for baptism. Already our dates are set for two years ahead.

"The simultaneous revival program is no longer an experiment. It has been proved. It waits only to be utilized."

Outline for Teacher

I. THE RESULTS OF PLANNING EVANGELISM THROUGH
   THE CHURCHES

II. THE EVANGELISM CHURCH COUNCIL ESSENTIAL IN
    PLANNING CHURCH REVIVALS

   1. Personnel
   2. When Does the Evangelism Council Meet?
   3. Duties of the Council
      (1) It is the church planning committee for
          evangelism
      (2) It is to institute methods for finding pros-
          pects for evangelistic efforts
      (3) It is to keep accurate records of prospects
      (4) It is to see that a class for new church mem-
          bers is conducted through the Training
          Union
   4. Advantages of Having the Evangelism Council

III. THE SIMULTANEOUS EVANGELISTIC CRUSADE

   1. What It Is
   2. Advantages of the Simultaneous Evangelistic
      Crusade
   3. It Should Be Conducted Annually
      (1) An annual crusade produces better results
      (2) A testimony

Questions for Thought and Discussion

1. Is the evangelism church council advisable for every church?
2. What are the advantages of two church revivals a year?
3. How does the simultaneous evangelistic crusade stimulate evangelism? Would it be helpful in promoting evangelism in your church?

4

Preparation for a Church Revival

THE supreme need of this hour is a heaven-sent revival in all of our churches. If every one of the churches in the Southern Baptist Convention would experience a genuine revival within the next year, it would start a conflagration of spiritual fervor and power that would sweep our nation and beyond. Such a spiritual movement would not be limited by boundary lines of nations.

Is it possible for every Southern Baptist church to have a real revival within a year? Yes. A genuine revival is within reach of every church. God will not withhold his blessings from any individual or church that will meet the conditions required by him.

I. WHAT IS A CHURCH REVIVAL?

A genuine church revival is not always determined by the number of decisions made or by the number of people added to the church. Such things are usually the fruits of a revival. A church revival is genuine when the members of the church are revived in their hearts.

An unusual example of a church revival took place in the Little Cussetah Baptist Church near Sapulpa, Oklahoma. The membership of this church is composed almost entirely of Creek Indians. The church was sixty-eight years old at the time of the revival. The pastor, whose name is Knaustaway Land, is a full-blooded Creek Indian. The author helped in the revival. Upon his arrival he was shown the names of prospects for church membership. The pastor then presented the evangelist with the names of forty-nine others. They might be termed backsliders. He called them prospects for restoration. They were people who were apparently living out of fellowship with God and the church. They had all practically quit attending church services, and many were living in known sin.

At the conclusion of the revival forty-eight of the forty-nine had been reclaimed by the church. In every case, without exception, a voluntary confession was made by the penitent "backslider," and the church voted to reclaim him just as it would vote to receive a new member. The result was that great power came upon the church. People of other nationalities began attending the services. The largest number ever baptized into the church in one year up to the time of the revival was eighteen. During this revival twenty-eight united with the church on profession of faith. This was a genuine church revival. There have been large ingatherings in revivals, with an amazing number of decisions, when the church was not revived. The revival in Little Cussetah Baptist Church was a genuine revival.

II. WHAT PRECEDES A CHURCH REVIVAL?

There is one thing that precedes all other elements which go with a church revival—that is desire. A genuine desire on the part of the pastor and the church, or at least on the part of the pastor, is an absolute essential if a revival is to be experienced. The first step in salvation on the part of a lost sinner is a desire on his part to be saved. God never coerces. The Philippian jailer who was so gloriously saved at midnight fell at the feet of Paul and Silas and said, "Sirs, what must I do to be saved?" (Acts 16: 30). The prodigal son did not receive the benediction of his father until that urge which sent his feet toward home came into his heart. God is not going to force a revival upon a church. The best evidence that a church needs a revival is that it does not want one.

Symptoms of a lack of desire are revealed when pastors and churches are hard to enlist in simultaneous crusades, or when no attempt is made to secure evangelistic help until shortly before the revival is to begin. The best symptom of a lack of desire for a revival is when a church wants to make the duration of its services as short as possible.

On the other hand, if the pastor has a deep desire for a revival, the victory is half won. If the pastor and the church have a burning desire for a revival, victory is assured. If the pastor and the church members are satisfied as they are, the evangelist who is to help, if he is sincere, is sure to have his heart broken.

One revival that will ever remain fixed in the memory of the author took place in a large city church. The pastor was so burdened for his cold and indifferent people that he could hardly pray audibly for weeping. Not only was the church revived, but there were more than a hundred and sixty additions to the church, with a hundred coming on profession of faith.

III. THE FIRST ESSENTIAL IN A CHURCH REVIVAL

There are a number of essential elements that help in bringing a genuine church revival. Chief among them is preparation. In fact, the author is convinced that preparation determines about 60 per cent of the results of a revival. He bases his conclusion upon experience and observation. Too many times a church depends almost entirely upon the reputation of the evangelist for results in a revival. This practice has become so general that churches seek frantically for men of reputation to conduct their revivals; and if they cannot get the evangelist they want, they just do not undertake the task of having a revival. Churches of this kind are blind as to their need. It is not a reputable preacher, one that can draw a crowd, that the church needs. It is proper and adequate preparation. Any compassionate-hearted gospel preacher can conduct a successful revival in a church that has made adequate preparation. In the majority of outstanding church revivals "ordinary" preachers did the preaching. Some of the biggest and most complete failures in revivals have come when a preacher of outstanding reputation did the preaching. The church was depending upon the evangelist, rather than upon God.

IV. WHAT CONSTITUTES ADEQUATE PREPARATION FOR A CHURCH REVIVAL?

The principal elements in adequate preparation for a church revival are now discussed.

1. *Set the Date Early*

Set the date for the revival far enough in advance to allow time for preparation. Many of our evangelistically minded churches set the dates from two to three years in advance. Every church should set its revival dates at least one year in advance.

2. *Secure Evangelistic Help*

Evangelistic help should be secured as soon as the date is set for the revival. Much prayer should be made for the leadership of the Holy Spirit in finding the man God would use to do the preaching. Capable evange- lists are dated far in advance; therefore, the church should seek its evangelistic help as early as possible. He may be the pastor. As soon as this matter is settled, then seek the counsel of the evangelist concerning his plans.

3. *Plan Adequate Publicity*

Publicize the revival. Let it be known to the mem- bership of the church and the community through the church bulletin, from the pulpit, and through the church organizations. Newspaper publicity is the best for the general public, whether the paper is a daily or a weekly publication. Use all the space it will give. Practically every church has some member who under- stands and properly evaluates publicity. Make him chairman of the publicity committee. Free publicity is the most effective. It gives spontaneity and a personal touch that no amount of paid advertising can give. If a radio station is accessible, use it for spot announce- ments. Efforts should be made to get the attention and interest of schools and civic organizations. There is no more important event in any community than a revival. There is little likelihood of reaching a whole community when nobody at school or in any of the service clubs knows that a revival is in progress.

Much of the publicity should be such that it can be read at a glance. People will not stop and read it. If it can be read at a glance, then the advertising will be noticed and read. Some suggested materials are store window cards, lapel buttons, and car bumper cards. (See display this chapter.) These items may be pur- chased from the Baptist Book Store in your area.

The best publicity is from lip to lip on the part of the members of the church, done by visitation, letter writing, casual conversation, by phone, or in any other way possible.

Publicity for a rural church is practically the same as that for a town or city church. Is there the same need for publicity in a rural community? Yes. During an election campaign the candidate will see to it that his picture is on every telephone pole and his card is placed in every home in the county. If this is good for a politician, how much more is it necessary in a revival where a church is trying to win souls to Christ! Sixty-six per cent of Southern Baptist churches are rural. They are all just as important in God's sight as churches elsewhere. They should place as much value on a revival as any city church does.

4. *Locate Prospects*

The next step is to locate prospects for the revival. This is a complex problem in most of our churches.

(1) *The Sunday school roll.*—The average church depends almost wholly upon its Sunday school roll for prospects for the revival. The Sunday school roll in the majority of our churches is depleted of prospects due to the intensified program of evangelism now being carried on by Southern Baptists.

One of the most timely movements ever initiated by Southern Baptists was the "Million More in '54" campaign by the Sunday school forces. The results of this effort have provided many thousands of prospects for revivals in our churches. But such an effort, mighty as it was, was not adequate for providing prospects for the future in soul-winning.

(2) *Use a visitor's card.*—Churches of medium size and up pass out visitors' cards in regular services and thereby keep a reasonable supply of names of prospects on hand. But churches with part-time preaching and

other small churches do not have many visitors in the
preaching service, and for that reason visitors' cards
are not used as a rule. A guest book for visitors to sign
is provided by many of the smaller churches. But
proper information is not obtainable in this manner
to determine whether or not the visitor is a prospect.
Many of the larger churches in the cities have opportunities to obtain names of new citizens from organizations which make such service a business. Regardless
of what method is used by a church to secure prospects
for the revival, there is one indispensable way for getting prospects. That way is the religious census.

(3) *The religious census.*—A census is imperative.
To obtain the best results, it should be taken thirty or
sixty days before the revival. Sunday afternoon is the
best time.

The importance of the census should be discussed
by the deacons. Sunday school officers and teachers,
Training Union leaders, Woman's Missionary Union
workers, laymen, and members of all the other organizations in the church should be committed to the plans
and should be willing to assist in every possible way.
The census is an all-church program and every organization in the church should co-operate.

a. The general leader.—Much care should be given
to the selection of the general leader. He should have
administrative ability, be willing to plan to the mi-
nutest detail, be thoroughly committed to the importance of the census, and should be willing to enter into
it with determination and enthusiasm.

The general leader should assign the territory. He
should make a careful study of the territory to be sur-
veyed and divide it into zones. A map of the territory
may be drawn showing the zones. The zones should be
numbered.

b. The zone leader.—A leader for each zone should be enlisted by the census director at least four weeks before the census. The same care should be taken in choosing these leaders as was suggested in selecting the general leader. The general leader should call a meeting of the zone leaders about four weeks preceding the census, at which time he will present to them a map of their zones and complete detailed information concerning their duties.

The zone leader must secure workers to cover his zone within two hours or less. In the average residential section one census taker for each block is sufficient. If there are large apartments or hotels, additional workers will be needed. On an average each zone leader will need approximately ten census takers. He should select these with care, realizing that the success of his work is dependent upon the faithfulness and efficiency of his helpers.

These workers will contact the people as representatives of the Lord and his church. They should therefore be consecrated, loyal, and intelligent members of the church. Each zone leader should have his helpers secured at least a week before the census. To fail here is to fail to get a good census. The workers should be informed when they are enlisted that on the day of the census they will be expected to remain at the church for lunch, instructions, and prayer. Everyone assisting must remain for this important hour.

c. Materials needed.—During the week preceding the census on Sunday, the zone leader should prepare the materials for each of his helpers. A sufficient number of census cards, instruction sheets, pencils, and other necessary materials should be placed in a large envelope for each census taker. A map of each block should be drawn on the outside of the envelope. The

census cards and the large envelopes may be secured
from the Baptist Book Store serving your area. All of
the materials should be on hand several weeks before
the census. Many times the taking of a census is handi-
capped because of insufficient materials with which to
work. The general leader should see that these are
provided.

d. *Taking the census*

(a) *The pastor.*—When the day arrives for taking
the census, the pastor should preach on some subject
that will emphasize the importance of such a survey.
A good text is John 4: 35, "Lift up your eyes, and look
on the fields; for they are white already to harvest."
The pastor will want to recognize the general leader,
zone leaders, and everyone who will assist in any way.
An expression of appreciation to workers will be helpful. Earnest prayer should be offered for divine guidance in such an important task.

(b) *Lunch.*—Immediately upon the conclusion of
the morning service a light lunch should be served to
all who are to assist and members of their families who
find it necessary to remain. The nursery should be
available for the small children of the census takers.
The workers should be ready to leave the church by
one o'clock. More people will be at home immediately
following lunch, and the workers will finish early in
the afternoon.

(c) *Information to census takers.*—As soon as lunch
is finished, those taking the census should be called together by the general leader for final instructions,
prayer, and fellowship. This meeting should not last
more than five or ten minutes. A brief meeting of the
workers in each zone should be held with the zone
leader in charge. The zone leader should present to
each census taker his envelope of materials, map, pen-

cils, and instructions. Each census taker should master the instructions and rules before going. He should know exactly where to go and what to do.

Two classes of people will be contacted by the census takers. Those who are possibilities and those who are not should be dealt with differently.

i. *Those who are not possibilities.*—This group includes people who are members of some other denomination, those who attend another church, or those who prefer another church. A hearty invitation should be extended these friends to visit the church when they are not engaged in their own services. One card should

---

CENSUS CARD
Use a Card for EACH Individual—Fill in EACH Blank

Name _____

Address _____

Age_____Date of Birth: Mo. _____Day_____Year_____

Sunday School Member: Yes___No___What School_____
                      Check which

Church Member: Yes___No___What Church_____
            Check which

Local Church Preference_____
  If no preference, write "None." If child under 9, enter parents' preference.

Denominational Preference_____
  If no preference, write "None." If child under 9, enter parents' preference.
FORM 675. BROADMAN SUPPLIES. NASHVILLE. TENNESSEE

---

be filled out for each individual. The card is illustrated here.

Census takers should be cautioned not to assume that certain people attend another church. Every home should be visited and the direct question asked. No exceptions should be made. Those of other denominations will appreciate this kind of visit, and the census taker will not be worked down securing information which will be destroyed or given to some other denomination which seldom, if ever, uses it. By the use of this method, much time will be conserved for use with those who are possibilities.

ii. *Those who are possibilities.*—Possibilities are un-churched Baptists, unsaved or unenlisted people who prefer the Baptist church, and those who express no preference. These are the real possibilities. Census takers should take plenty of time with these and secure detailed information. Census takers should remember to use a card for each individual, and to write only one name on a card. They should not guess. They should do the writing themselves. They should be accurate and write plainly. They should fill out every blank on the card, or the information will be incomplete and useless. They should be thorough. They should get the exact age of each individual—date of birth, month, and year, if possible. They should see that initials and names are correct. They should check on the street address carefully. If it is an apartment or hotel, the room number should be given. Census takers should stick to their own territory and not miss anybody.

When there is no one at home, a card should be filled out giving the address and indicating that no one is at home. When the territory is covered, census takers should return to the church and leave their cards with the person responsible for compiling the information. The zone leaders should arrange with workers to follow up on the not-at-home cards on Monday.

5. *Using the Information Secured*

The information which has been secured is of little value, and no lasting good will come from the work, unless it is used, and used quickly.

(1) *Using the information in the Sunday school*
a. Assort information.—Sufficient help should be se-

cured Monday following the census to assort, grade, and tabulate the information. This should be completed by Wednesday night and placed in the hands of the officers and teachers of the Sunday school and others who are interested in soul-winning.

b. Grade the information.—The information should be graded according to the plan of the Sunday school, by departments and classes. In many cases new departments and classes should be organized and additional workers secured to go after the possibilities.

c. Tabulate the information.—Several copies of the information should be provided. Teachers, department officers, general officers, and pastor should have a copy of the possibilities by classes and departments. This will require considerable work, but it is necessary if the information is to be used effectively. Information should be in the hands of the Sunday school workers and other soul-winners by Wednesday night following the census on Sunday.

(2) *Using the information in the Training Union.* —The names of all Baptists in the community who have not transferred their membership to the church should be assigned as prospects to the Training Union.

(3) *Using the information in the revival meeting.*— One of the most effective ways to use the information in a revival meeting is through the Sunday school. If these possibilities are enlisted in Sunday school, taught the Word of God, and led by consecrated teachers and officers, they will most likely find the Lord and a place in his church. However, there are additional ways in which this information may be used in soul-winning.

a. The unenlisted Baptists.—A typewritten list of all of the unenlisted Baptists living in the territory should be prepared, with names, addresses, and places of membership. A warm, cordial letter from the pastor

Evangelistic Crusade Campaign Materials

BAPTIST *Simultaneous* REVIVALS

● YOU ARE INVITED BY 29,500 CHURCHES
● SOUTHERN BAPTIST CONVENTION WIDE

Christ Is The Answer

Come unto me, all ye that labour...and I will give you rest.

1

BAPTIST *Simultaneous* REVIVALS

DATE

2

Description of Materials

1. Billboard Poster—9½ x 19½ feet, $6.00 each; 5 or more, $5.00 each

2. Cloth Street Banner—3 x 12 feet, $8.50 each; 5 or more $7.50 each

Evangelistic Crusade Campaign Materials

3

6

7

8

4   5

9

Description of Materials

3. Window Card—13½ x 20½ inches, 50, $5.25; 100, $10.00

4. Blotter—5½ x 3½ inches, 100, $1.00; 500, $4.75; 1000, $9.00

5. Post Card—100, 75¢; 500, $3.00; 1000, $5.00

6. Day-Glo Bumper Sticker—15 x 4 inches, 25, $3.50; 50, $6.50; 100, $12.00

7. Sunday School Attendance Chain—500, 80¢; 1000, $1.50

8. Lapel Button—100, 75¢; 500, $3.25; 1000, $6.00

9. Day-Glo Arrows—12 x 6 inches, 1 pair, 10¢; 10 or more pairs, 9¢ a pair

to these fellow-Baptists will be helpful. These same names should be placed on cards for use in personal visitation by the pastor and other workers. One of the most challenging tasks in evangelism facing Baptists today is the enlistment of the Lord's people in his work.

b. The unsaved.—Typewritten copies of these should be prepared both on paper and on individual cards. A letter to the unsaved immediately following the census will be helpful. These names will furnish the pastor, the evangelist, and other workers an abundance of information needed for personal visitation and personal soul-winning. The pastor may preach on the fields that are white unto harvest and point out the multitudes that were discovered in the census.

6. *The Association-wide Religious Census*

In all associational simultaneous crusades a religious census is imperative if a maximum of results is to be obtained. Many problems arise in taking an association-wide census, sometimes reaching a point of seriousness between churches and pastors, due to division of territory and unfortunate attitudes toward proselyting. Here is an outline for taking an association-wide census that, if adhered to, will avoid all such problems.

(1) *Appoint a committee.*—Appoint an associational census committee with a chairman who is experienced and duly qualified to direct the work.

(2) *Divide the association into zones.*—Divide into zones the territory to be taken, without regard to location of churches.

(3) *Determine census takers needed.*—The census committee should arrive at the total number of census takers needed. Each church should be expected to

supply its quota of census workers on the basis of church membership as recorded in associational minutes.

(4) *Rally for census takers.*—Conduct an associational rally for all census takers on Sunday afternoon one week before the census is taken. At this rally recognize representative groups from each church, announce zone leaders, and have some to speak on how to take the census and how to use it according to the adopted plan.

(5) *Deliver census cards.*—Appoint another associational committee composed of laymen and women to divide and to deliver census cards according to the following plan:

Separate cards with names of all who are members of local churches and turn these cards over to churches to which they belong.

Separate cards with names of nonresident Baptists who express local church preference and cards with names of all unsaved who express local Baptist church preference, and turn them over to church they prefer.

Make a master tabulation of all nonresident Baptists who express no local church preference and all unsaved who express Baptist preference with no particular choice of a church or no preference at all. Give a copy to each church co-operating in the crusade.

This is a fair and equitable plan for every church. If followed, it will leave no well-founded excuse for misunderstandings or controversies.

V. A WEEK OF PRAYER

The entire week preceding the revival should be planned as a week of prayer. This is basic. The lack of prayer is the weakest point in church life. There never was a genuine revival that was not preceded by prayer.

1. *Cottage Prayer Meetings*

Plan cottage prayer meetings to be conducted on Monday, Tuesday, Thursday, and Friday nights. The reason for naming so many nights is that some who cannot attend on one night may be able to attend on another. Secure the church roll and divide the church membership into districts. Each district should comprise at least twelve church homes. Secure a home in each district where a prayer meeting may be held. Then secure a leader for each prayer meeting. Publish this in the church bulletin, or in some way get the program into the hands of all resident church members. Announce clearly the time, place, and leader of each meeting to be held. Ask that devotionals be brief and that much time be spent in prayer for the revival, the church members, the pastor, the evangelist, the singer, the choir, lost loved ones, friends, Sunday school pupils, and neighbors. Ask that they pray definitely for a special visitation of the Holy Spirit.

2. *All-Church Prayer Meetings*

The committee should arrange for an all-church prayer meeting to be conducted on Wednesday evening. The pastor and his staff of workers should put forth the best effort possible to have a large attendance present at this service. Set out to have one or more representatives from each home present. A program is suggested for this service:

(1) *Recognize the family groups present.*—Have all Sunday school workers and pupils to stand for recognition. Then recognize the Training Union, the Woman's Missionary Society, and the Brotherhood.

(2) *Have a testimony meeting.*—Have each person to stand and state at what age he was saved, where he

was saved, and what person was most responsible for leading him to Christ. Be strict in holding every person to a testimony of these three things only. If not, then some will make long talks and no time will be left for prayer. The object in testifying to these three points is obvious. The first point will bring out the fact that most people are saved in early childhood. This has a tendency to offset a widespread doubt on the part of parents about child conversion. The second point will reveal that people are won to Christ in the home by a mother, father, or some other relative; that some are won by Sunday school teachers in the classroom or by personal effort on the part of a friend. It will be seen that a vast majority are won to Christ during a revival. All this stimulates interest, enlightens the people, and provokes effort. Of course, there are many other splendid and effective methods of getting people to testify.

(3) *Give time for requests for prayer.*—Spend as much time as practical in earnest prayer for requests made and for every interest of the revival. Close with a good song and an invitation for confession of Christ, for church membership, or for rededication of life.

In addition to this, have a chain of prayer on the Saturday before the revival begins and each Saturday while the revival is in session. Begin at 7:00 A.M. and close at 7:00 P.M. Urge initiative on the part of all the churches in the matter of prayer.

VI. a good prayer program for a church revival

Cottage prayer meetings and other prayer meetings should be held the week before the revival begins. At least one cottage prayer meeting should be held for every fifteen church members. For example, a church with one hundred members or less would need to plan for at least eight prayer meetings, holding two each night on Monday, Tuesday, Thursday, and Friday. For churches with three hundred members, it would be necessary to have five cottage prayer meetings each of the four nights. In a church of twelve hundred members there would be a need of twenty each night, etc.

Prayer meetings should be held in various sections of the community according to where the church members live.

Secure permission to hold cottage prayer meetings in the homes of your members or, where possible, in the homes of the unsaved of the community.

If there are apartment buildings in your territory, it might be wise to schedule several prayer meetings, perhaps one on each floor and invite all who live on that floor to attend.

It is of vital importance that places of meetings should be arranged early.

1. *Choose the Leaders Well in Advance*

Use men, women, and young people from your church membership. If possible, the leader should not be the one in whose home the prayer meeting is held.

2. *Print the Schedule*

Print in the church bulletin or mimeograph on a separate sheet the schedule of cottage prayer meetings, giving the homes, addresses, and leaders for each night. State that church families are expected to attend services nearest them.

3. *Assign Responsibility*

Assign responsibility of contacting church members and unsaved people in each area, inviting them to attend the prayer meetings. If necessary, arrange transportation.

4. *Provide Adequate Instructions*

Call a meeting of your cottage prayer meeting leaders as soon as possible in order that they may be given adequate instructions and suggestions as to program and detailed plans for each cottage prayer meeting. The following suggestions should be considered.

Start on time.

Be sure that everyone has met all who are present.

Have a seating arrangement to make everyone feel that he is a part of the group.

Use the Bible, responsive readings, Scripture references read in unison, individuals reading certain passages, and quotations from memory.

Make the Bible reading purposeful, but do not make this a Bible lesson instead of a prayer meeting. Be sure to present the plan of salvation. Study God's command to witness, his promises to his followers, and how Jesus and his disciples witnessed to those around him. Ask all who attend to bring Bibles.

Plan for the appropriate use of hymns.

Lead those present to share Christian experiences.

If it is possible, from the church census, Sunday school rolls, and other sources, prepare a list of unsaved and unchurched according to the areas of the community. Give these names to the leader of that particular area so that there may be prayer for them in the cottage prayer meetings. It is entirely possible that those who attend cottage prayer meetings would want to visit one of these prospects at the close of the prayer meeting hour.

Give an opportunity for additional requests for prayer.

Lead in a season of prayer and ask those who are present to participate. Several may be asked to pray for specific requests, and there may be periods of silent prayer.

Have several seasons of prayer rather than just one. For example, you may have Scripture passages on the individual's responsibility and then pray for those who will witness. Another season of prayer may be for the lost, and a third for the unchurched. Another season of prayer would be for your pastor, the visiting evangelist, the singer, etc.

Have another season of prayer for the homes of your church and community.

Pray and expect results. Sincere and earnest prayer will change the lives of those present and lead them to witness to the unsaved and unenlisted in the community.

5. *Other Prayer Suggestions*

Pause at noon. Secure personal commitments from church members who will promise to pause at noon daily for prayer one week prior to and during the revival.

Seek to enlist every member of the church to attend the special midweek prayer service the Wednesday prior to the beginning of your revival.

If your church plans a Saturday round-the-clock day of prayer, co-operate fully in enlisting all members to be present sometime during the prayer schedule.

For one month in all organizations of the church at every meeting time there should be a pause for prayer for the revival and the unsaved.

With your leaders think through every possible opportunity where the people can be led to do more praying than ever before. It is of vital importance that every member of your church be led to realize the absolute necessity of prayer and more prayer.

Outline for Teacher

I. what is a church revival?

II. what precedes a church revival?

III. the first essential in a church revival

IV. what constitutes adequate preparation for a church revival?

    1. Set the Date Early

    2. Secure Evangelistic Help

    3. Plan Adequate Publicity

    4. Locate Prospects

        (1) The Sunday school roll

        (2) Use a visitor's card

        (3) The religious census

    5. Using the Information Secured

        (1) Using the information in the Sunday school

        (2) Using the information in the Training Union

        (3) Using the information in the revival meeting

    6. The Association-wide Religious Census

        (1) Appoint committee

        (2) Divide the association into zones

        (3) Determine census takers needed

        (4) Rally for census takers

        (5) Deliver census cards

V. a week of prayer

    1. Cottage Prayer Meetings

2. All-Church Prayer Meetings
    (1) Recognize the family groups present
    (2) Have a testimony meeting
    (3) Give time for requests for prayer

VI. A GOOD PRAYER PROGRAM FOR A CHURCH REVIVAL
    1. Choose the Leaders Well in Advance
    2. Print the Schedule
    3. Assign Responsibility
    4. Provide Adequate Instructions
    5. Other Prayer Suggestions

Questions for Thought and Discussion

1. What are the best publicity media for advertising the revival?

2. What mistakes should a church avoid in taking a religious census?

3. Outline an effective prayer program in preparation for a revival.

5

Performance in a Revival

THE best way not to have a successful revival in a church is to follow the line of least resistance. That probably accounts for many a failure in churches, whether it be a revival or anything else the church should undertake. A church can set a date for a revival, invite an evangelist to do the preaching, publicize the meeting, proceed with prayer meetings, and then utterly fail to reach people for Christ. Why? Because no definite plans were made ahead of time for making the revival succeed. The preceding chapter leads up to the beginning of the revival only. The performance during the revival is just as essential as the preparation. What is to be done during the two weeks' effort which has been planned for?

I. HOW MANY SERVICES EACH DAY?

Many churches have only evening services during a revival. In such instances the morning services are dispensed with "to allow people to visit in the interest of the revival" or for other reasons. There have been a few successful revivals where only one service each day, except Sunday, was held. It could be possible that conditions would be such that it would be best to have only one service each weekday, but such cases are certainly exceptions. The church that, for no good reason, dispenses with morning services during its revival has robbed itself of a rich blessing. It is difficult to have a large attendance in a religious service on weekday mornings, but here are some advantages of the morning service:

It affords an opportunity for the evangelist to teach the Bible in a fashion that is not practical at night.

It is essential that church members be edified and built up in the faith. This can be done in the morning services much better than it can in the evening services.

It is a known fact that many people who cannot attend services at night can attend morning services because of working conditions, home duties, old age, etc.

There is essentially more spiritual power in the evening service if it is preceded by a good spiritual morning service.

In many revivals which the author has conducted, morning services (except Saturday) have borne tremendous fruit in the salvation of the lost as well as in additions by letter.

II. AT WHAT HOUR SHOULD MORNING SERVICES BE CONDUCTED?

The answer is: Set the time that is most practical, based on local conditions. The following are the three periods most widely used:

7:00 to 7:45 A.M. Results: The highest attendance of any period (in city and town churches) with little visible results.

12:00 noon to 12:55 P.M., with luncheon served. Those who choose to eat pay for their meals. Results: A good attendance with meager visible results.

10:00 to 11:00 A.M. Attendance varies from very small to around two hundred in medium-sized and larger churches. Results: In many cases, wonderful in conversions and additions by letter. This is the most practical time for rural churches. Regardless of where a church is located, this hour affords a much better opportunity for members to drive by homes of prospects and others and bring them to church. It also generally eliminates the spirit of hurry.

Attendance at these morning services can be stimulated by assigning to the Sunday school or the W.M.U. the sponsorship of attendance. A blackboard record of group attendance may be kept.

III. MUSIC IN THE REVIVAL

Herein lies one of the most controversial problems now existing in Southern Baptist churches. This book is not written for the purpose of suppressing the ideas or the convictions of anyone. The sole purpose of this book is to share with others the value of experience gained by the author from a ministry devoted to church evangelism. The author is not a musician. He can give to others only what he has learned from close observation as to the effect of different types of music in evangelism. He can say without fear of contradiction that music can be of tremendous help in a revival, second only in value to the preaching of the Word. Or music can all but wreck the effectiveness of great preaching in a revival. Any evangelist who has served with a degree of success will bear this testimony: The best music in a revival is gospel music that is familiar to the largest number of people in the congregation and which, of course, will result in the participation of a maximum number of people in the singing.

Another observation of the author is this: It is just as essential for the people in the congregation to understand the message and the words of a song as it is for them to understand the message and the words of the sermon. Most of the song leaders in Southern

Baptist churches are volunteers from the congregation.
This is because about twenty thousand of our churches
are rural and few of these are blessed with a paid musician as leader. The employed ministers of music are
like preachers—they are products of some school. They
will likely use the type of music that they were taught
in the schools where they received training.

1. *The Value of Gospel Music in Revivals* [1]

The value of gospel music in evangelism is an ex-
haustless theme upon which we dare not dwell. Often-
times the gospel may tell its melting story in vain to
a sin-hardened heart, when some simple gospel hymn
like an arrow will pierce that heart and cause it to
yield to Christ.

Salvation and song are twins. Great revivals have
ridden on the crest of sacred song throughout the ages.
Dwight L. Moody once said that Ira D. Sankey sang
more people back to God than he ever preached back
to God. From the standpoint of revival services, great
gospel singing stands second only to the evangelistic
sermon in importance. This writer has never experienced a great revival without great singing.

If the revival music is to be effective, a number
of important matters need consideration—the song
leader, the pianist, the choir, the right type of music,
the song service, the purpose of singing the gospel.

(1) *The song leader.*—In most churches it is wise to
secure a song leader from outside the church. Too
many churches are prone to use home talent when a
new leader is definitely needed. The song leader
should be a loyal, consecrated Christian. He should

---

[1] This discussion of music in revivals is by the late Dr. B. B. Mc-
Kinney, a widely recognized authority in this field. It is taken from
The Southern Baptist Program of Evangelism, by C. E. Matthews.

have a sincere love in his heart for all people. He should love gospel music above all other types of music. The relationship between the pastor, evangelist, and song leader should be one of mutual confidence and Christian cordiality. The song leader should at all times recognize and respect the evangelist or pastor-evangelist as leader of the revival. He should never assume authority that belongs to the evangelist. However, the wise pastor or evangelist will never usurp the powers and privileges of the song leader by exercising a domineering spirit. The song leader is to have complete charge of the musical program in the campaign, co-operating always with the evangelist.

The ideal song leader is one who will carry the burden of lost souls upon his heart, one who is capable of leading a congregation in a happy soul-stirring song service, and of organizing the musical program in such a way as properly to prepare the congregation for the message of the evangelist. In addition to leading the congregational singing, the song leader should be able to organize and direct large choirs and to lead prayer meetings, soul-winning bands, and decision services. It is not absolutely essential that the song leader be a soloist. The things already mentioned are far more important.

(2) *The pianist.*—Pianos are more desirable for revivals than organs. The outstanding song leaders of the past used pianos. They found that the quick incisive notes of a piano held the singing of a large congregation together far better than did the organ. However, two well-tuned pianos with an organ make a fine combination for the larger auditoriums. An organ and piano combination for the average sized auditorium is acceptable, but two pianos are more effective.

If an organ is used with the piano, the pianist should take the lead by playing the introductions to the songs, thus setting the tempo necessary for live evangelistic singing. The instruments should be placed where the accompanists can see the song leader at all times.

Pianists and organists who are not heartily in sympathy with evangelistic work should never be selected to play for revivals.

The pianist should be a consecrated Christian and should always understand that he is under the direction not only of the song leader but of the evangelist as well. Fortunate indeed is the song leader who has an efficient pianist, for he can make or mar the song services. Playing hymns and gospel songs is an art within itself. Conservatory training does not necessarily qualify one for intelligent playing of gospel music. Hymns and gospel songs require a spiritual touch which is not required in other forms of piano playing. The pianist should be able to read music readily and accurately. He should possess a keen sense of rhythm, the ability to memorize, and willingness to follow the song leader implicitly. The song leader and the pianist should be on hand well in advance of every service. It is always best to use the same pianist throughout the revival. This will prove to be of great benefit to the song leader and to the services.

(3) *The choir.*—A church will get out of a revival what it puts into it. If any church is to receive the largest possible return, it must begin weeks in advance the work of preparation, prayer, and organization. Every church should make special musical preparation for the coming revival. A revival choir is a decided asset provided the audience does not allow the choir to carry the burden of the singing.

The mission of the choir is to stimulate congregational singing, to assist the audience in learning new hymns, and to provide special music. The revival choir should be organized and thoroughly trained well in advance of the revival meeting. The church should appoint a committee composed of people who are vitally interested in revivals to make a complete survey of the music talent of all departments of the church, taking the names of those who will pledge themselves as choir members for the revival. By all means, enlist as many in the revival choir as possible. Have them sign pledge cards that they will be faithful to God and the services.

Following this work every member of the choir should be invited to a choir supper for fellowship, organization, prayer, and instruction. It would be well to plan for several rehearsals prior to the opening of the revival. Attractive new songs and choruses should be rehearsed for the revival. These meetings should be seasoned with earnest prayer and dedication. In most places the local church music leader can conduct these rehearsals. By all means, all choir members should be contacted by letter and by phone several times preceding the revival. During the revival the song leader should have some special rehearsals following the evening services. This is a good time to prepare special numbers which will be sung on the following evening.

The revival chorus choir should be composed of adults and young people who love the Lord and the unsaved. If at all possible, an Intermediate and a Junior choir should be organized and used during the revival. Some church buildings do not have room on the platform for a large chorus choir. When this is the problem, the church will find that it is well worth whatever trouble and expense may be involved to provide a special platform to take care of the choir.

(4) *The right type of music.*—Many churches are
satisfied with the usual Sunday morning music for
evangelistic services. We need to get out of the usual
into the unusual. There is a vast difference between a
worship service and an evangelistic service. The regular worship service is primarily for Christians; the
evangelistic service is for the unsaved. The songs and
sermons are directed to the unsaved. Christians who
are present should be there to assist in the services by
their prayers, their singing, and their personal work.
A revival demands a different type of music. We must
have gospel music that will produce results—evangelistic results; gospel music that will turn sinners to God
and eternal life. The old formal hymns are good in
their place, but their place is not in revivals. In their
stead are needed the bright militant gospel songs with
a burning evangelistic message. We need to magnify
the old favorite gospel songs that our Christian fathers
and mothers sang in the home and the Sunday school.
Then the new songs and choruses can be used very
effectively. The world needs new spiritual songs as it
needs new spiritual sermons.

There is no place in evangelistic work for anthems
and classical numbers. All special music by the choir
and others should be gospel songs or special gospel
song arrangements. Every song should contain a vital
message.

In every revival there should be an ample supply
of good songbooks. The church hymnal of the average
church can be satisfactorily used provided such church
hymnal contains a sufficient number of popular gospel
songs. The formal hymnal was never intended for revival meetings.

(5) *The song service.*—The musical portion of an
evangelistic service is tremendously important. Each

song service should be made so interesting that it will add immeasurably to the drawing power of the service; so inspiring that multitudes will be drawn to God's house and to the foot of the cross. In order to accomplish this, ample time should be given to the song service. It is not a question of how soon the singing can be brought to a close. All must realize that music is an instrument of God and that there must be time to magnify it.

The service should begin with a piano prelude or a good orchestra number. This will call the people to their places and will help to quiet the congregation. This prelude should begin some five minutes before the time for the singing to begin. Classical and secular numbers are utterly out of place here. Familiar hymns and gospel songs are altogether appropriate.

The congregational singing should be joyful and spontaneous, but never jazzy. The song service is no place for light-heartedness and cheap jokes. This is the time to create a warm spiritual atmosphere for the whole service. After the congregational singing come the announcements and offering. The offertory played by the pianist or orchestra should be a gospel song and never a classical or secular piece. Often the spiritual atmosphere is lost because of the change to this type of music.

The special music, whether by choir or otherwise, should be left entirely in the hands of the song leader. He is held responsible unto God for every special number. It is not always advisable to use local talent for solos and other special songs. Here the song leader will need to be careful. It is far better, if the leader has a solo voice, for him to sing these solos. All special songs should contain a mighty appeal to the lost or to the redeemed.

The best singing of all should be on the invitation song. This song, as far as possible, should fit the message of the hour and should be sung with a prayer for lost people. It should always be sung pleadingly and brightly, not in a dull funeral-dirge tempo.

(6) *The purpose of singing the gospel.*—The purpose of singing the gospel is not to entertain; the purpose of all singing in evangelism should be to lead lost souls into the fold of God. The right kind of singing prepares the way for the message of the evangelist. Every song used should lead people a step higher toward God.

There is no place in revivals for a choir member or soloist to show off his voice. All must sing for the glory of God.

IV. PRAYER DURING A CHURCH REVIVAL

Prayer during preparation for a revival has been discussed in another chapter. But praying must not stop when revival services begin. It is much easier to intensify prayer when it is accompanied by preaching than it is when there is no preaching being done. Prayer and preaching support each other. A program of prayer during a revival is very essential.

There should be a prayer meeting by Sunday school departments for a period of thirty minutes before the evening services during weekdays. In small churches these prayer groups may be reduced to one for men, one for women, and one for young people. In every case, qualified leaders for each group should be selected ahead of time by the pastor or by an appointed prayer chairman. The morning service, if conducted from 10:00 A.M. to 11:00 A.M., should be preceded by a thirty minute prayer meeting under the leadership of the pastor. Have a thirty minute chain of prayer going on from 7:00 A.M. to 7:00 P.M. on each Saturday during the revival, at least two persons praying at each period. Those who pray may do so in the home or at the church, preferably at the church. These prayer meetings have saved many revivals. A prayerless revival is a powerless revival.

The author conducted a revival in a city church. He was informed by the pastor that practically all of the prospects for the revival were members of the Junior departments of the Sunday school. The pastor said, "There are a few adult men that we have had on our prospect list for years, but they seldom attend church." The situation as described by the pastor proved to be correct. A group of consecrated men, some five or six, met for a thirty minute prayer service each evening preceding the preaching service. The names of the unsaved men which had been before the church were interceded for in earnest and fervent prayer in each service. Again and again the men in the prayer group would beseech God in tears, calling the names of these men one by one as they prayed. Every man on the list was saved before the meeting closed. Among them were the fire chief, the chief of police, and a man in the employ of the government who was a brother of the chairman of the deacons. Prayer is the answer for power in a revival, and by all means praying should be specific.

V. PREACHING IN A CHURCH REVIVAL

The value of preaching in the salvation of a lost world must never be minimized. God ordained it that way. "For after that in the wisdom of God the world by wisdom knew not God, it pleased God by the foolishness of preaching to save them that believe" (1 Cor. 1:21). The preaching in a revival is something over

which the members of the church have no control
except to pray for the one who has this vital responsibility. Prayer for the evangelist and not criticism of
him is what makes the evangelist effective. The evangelist, as a rule, should include the cardinal doctrines
of the Bible in his messages as the Holy Spirit leads
him. Repentance, heaven, hell, sin, and the new birth
should be greatly emphasized, and the exaltation of
Christ should be primal in every message. Plenty of
time should be given to the appeal at the close of each
revival service, if the evangelist feels so impressed.

VI. THE PASTOR AS HIS OWN EVANGELIST

With present-day conditions that make church attendance so difficult and with alluring temptations on
every side causing backsliding and low moral stand-
ards on the part of church members, it is absolutely
necessary that churches have two revivals each year to
prevent deplorable apostasy. Who is going to conduct
all of these revivals? There are only a few full-time
evangelists in comparison with revival needs. This presents a real problem. The answer is that every pastor
ought to conduct at least one revival in his own church
every year. The pastors of many churches do this. In
fact, the pastors of our greatest churches have done this
for years. May this not be the reason, in part at least,
why these are great churches and why these pastors
stay so long with them? There is no other thing that
will bring the pastor so close to his people or his people
so close to him as his conducting a revival in his own
church. People who are saved under the preaching of
a minister will always have a warm spot in their hearts
for him. They feel different toward him than toward
any other preacher. He is more than a pastor to them,
and they are more than just church members to him.

Many ministers do not conduct revivals in their own pastorates. They think the people need to hear new voices. It is profitable for the people to hear a new voice occasionally. Two revivals each year, with the pastor conducting one and a guest evangelist the other, make a well-balanced program. The other reason is that many pastors think it is necessary for them to preach new sermons in a revival. That is definitely a mistaken idea. In revivals, preach over and over the sermons that God blesses. The late Dr. George W. Truett preached some of his revival sermons over and over in his church for more than thirty years. The people who hid those sermons in their hearts through hearing them so many times were indeed rich. The inner strength that came from his accumulation of gospel truth fortified them against temptation.

The author preached a sermon entitled "Life's Supreme Decision" in twenty-three revivals in Travis Avenue Baptist Church, Fort Worth, Texas. God blessed this sermon more the last time it was preached than he did the first time. Dr. R. G. Lee has preached his great sermon, "Pay Day Some Day," more than five hundred times. He has preached it at least one time every year in his own church during his long ministry there. Every time he preaches it, he has an overflow congregation. We sing the same songs over and over. A person may have heard "Amazing Grace" a thousand times and love it better every time he hears it. What is true of a genuine gospel song is true of a genuine gospel sermon.

VII. PERSONAL WORK DURING A CHURCH REVIVAL

It is becoming more and more evident that most of the people who are won to Christ during a revival are contacted by a personal soul-winner at some time

somewhere before they respond to the appeal of the
evangelist and make a public confession of Christ before the church. This does not mean that the preaching of the gospel is becoming ineffective. Were it not
for the preaching of the gospel, few people would do
personal work and very few people would make decisions. Preaching is seed sowing. Preaching creates
atmosphere. Preaching inspires the Christian to wit-

Prospect ....Age ....

Address ....Phone ....

Personal Worker ....Date ....

Address ....Phone ....

Class ....Dept. ....

CONDITION OF PROSPECT	REPORT
.... Lost ....Interested	.... Made Visit ....Interested
.... Has been in services	.... Had Prayer ....Read Bible
.... Member of this Sunday School	.........Made Profession
.... Member of this Church	.........Will join this Church
.... Unaffiliated Baptist	.... Will join ....Church
.... Christian but not Church Member	.... Will join this Sunday School
.... Should be in Sunday School	.........Send for letter

(Over)

PROSPECT CARD FOR VISITATION EVANGELISM

Check (√) the agency that should receive credit for this visit:

☐ Sunday School

☐ Training Union

☐ Woman's Missionary Union

☐ Brotherhood

E 1 Broadman Supplies

ness, and preaching of the right sort points the people to the lifted-up Christ. "And I, if I be lifted up from the earth, will draw all men unto me" (John 12: 32).

Plan for personal work. Here is the most important phase of a church revival if results are to be expected. Definite planning and definite carrying out of plans are absolutely essential. Announcements by the pastor such as "Everyone bring one" are not specific and will not get the job done. Great preaching by a "crowd-drawing" preacher accompanied by a great choir and soul-stirring music will not allure many unbelievers to the services. It takes good planning and well-executed plans in personal work to have great results in a revival. Here are plans that will work.

Have the names of plenty of prospects on hand. Have the names with addresses written on cards, like the sample on page 70. (These cards may be purchased at any Baptist Book Store. Price 40¢ for 100, $1.75 for 500, $3.25 for 1,000.)

Have "after services" in which these prospect names will be given out to members of the church to visit. You may wish to give these cards out at every service. Do not give more than three names at one time to each visitor. Give instructions on how to visit and request that all cards with names of prospects contacted be returned to the pastor or some other designated person each day, without fail.

During the service the personal worker should, if at all possible, sit by the prospect he has visited. Pray constantly that the Holy Spirit may do his work while the sermon is being preached. When the invitation is given, if the prospect lingers, speak a word of encouragement to him—something like this, "I would be happy to walk with you to the front, for God has spoken to you out of his Word." You will discover, in

many instances, that this courteous and kindly suggestion is all that is needed. Do not let fear defeat your
witnessing.

Outline for Teacher

    I. HOW MANY SERVICES EACH DAY?

    II. AT WHAT HOUR SHOULD MORNING SERVICES BE CON-
        DUCTED?

    III. MUSIC IN THE REVIVAL
        1. The Value of Gospel Music in Revivals
            (1) The song leader
            (2) The pianist
            (3) The choir
            (4) The right type of music
            (5) The song service
            (6) The purpose of singing the gospel

    IV. PRAYER DURING A CHURCH REVIVAL

    V. PREACHING IN A CHURCH REVIVAL

    VI. THE PASTOR AS HIS OWN EVANGELIST

    VII. PERSONAL WORK DURING A CHURCH REVIVAL

Questions for Thought and Discussion

1. Compare the advantages and the disadvantages of
   weekday morning services in a revival.
2. What is the best time for the morning service?
3. Outline the most important suggestions regarding
   revival music.
4. List on the blackboard an adequate program of
   prayer and personal work during the revival.

6

Using Church Organizations
the First Week of the Revival

I. EVERY REVIVAL SHOULD LAST TWO WEEKS

The revival effort in Southern Baptist churches varies as to duration. The department of evangelism of the Home Mission Board recommends that church revivals be of two weeks' duration. There are several reasons for this.

A unified program for churches must include time as well as methods. The simultaneous revival method that has become so universally popular and so marvelously effective requires standardization as to length of participation. Concerted effort is impossible unless length of participation is the same on the part of the churches. The entire program is built on the premise of two weeks' duration because an overwhelming majority of the churches have adopted the two weeks' revival effort as being the most practical.

Co-operation is essential. The autonomy of a New Testament church is acknowledged and adopted in the mind and practice of every real Baptist. Along with this belief is a conviction as deep as the soul in every true Baptist, that the principle of voluntary co-operation demands more of the grace of God for the individual than it does to conform to any legal document. It is that principle and that belief that keeps Southern Baptists together in their effort to evangelize the world. The Southern Baptist Convention itself exercises no authority over any church or individual. The convention is composed of duly elected messengers from co-operating churches. Its decisions and its recommendations never go beyond the principle of voluntary acceptance and participation on the part of the churches. But it is expected by all that a true Baptist will abide by the will of the majority whether he is in hearty agreement with its action or not.

This idea is scriptural. The true believer bowed to the will of the majority in both the Old and the New Testaments.

Convention actions should be known and taken seriously. No action of the Southern Baptist Convention carries with it a guarantee of infallibility; however, the principle that has been followed by churches throughout the history of the Convention is to abide by its recommendations. Add to this tradition the seriousness of the times in which we live.

II. THE SOUTHERN BAPTIST PROGRAM OF EVANGELISM

Every Baptist ought to read, to understand, and to consider seriously the Southern Baptist program of evangelism as recommended by the Southern Baptist Convention in its session in St. Louis, Missouri, in 1947, and ratified in its 1948 session in Memphis, Tennessee.

"John L. Slaughter, Alabama, chairman of the committee on evangelism, presented the report for his committee which was adopted with the following recommendations:

"That the states, associations, and churches continue to concentrate on the program of evangelism as set forth by the Southern Baptist Convention, which is the New Testament plan of worldwide evangelism.

The success of this program and the extent of its reach depend upon the co-operative endeavor of every denominational leader, of every church organization, and of all the members of our local churches.

"That we continue to be sympathetic toward, and increase our emphasis on, mass evangelism and personal evangelism. We realize that one cannot succeed apart from the other. This comprises a call to enlist the fullest co-operation of all our missionaries at home and abroad.

"That the many modern, scientific discoveries in the field of communications, such as radio, visual education, etc., shall be utilized more than ever. Recognition is hereby expressed in the joyous progress of the Baptist Radio Hour and in the pictures made by the associational missionaries of the work in the rural areas.

"Being aware of the progress that has been made in the states where the department of evangelism has been organized, and in accord with the program of the Home Mission Board's department of evangelism, we furthermore urge:

"That a department of evangelism should be created in each state as early as possible.

"That a superintendent of evangelism should be elected to lead in this work in the various states.

"That the executive board of the associations shall continue to elect annually two officers—an organizer and a chairman of evangelism.

"That the program committee of the district associations, on the order of business, provide a prominent place on the program for the discussion of evangelism.

"That the local church shall elect a committee on evangelism composed of representatives of the departments of the church, viz., Sunday school, Training

Union, W.M.U., and Brotherhood. This over-all committee will plan and promote evangelism in the church
in view of its large soul-winning opportunities.

"That we give larger emphasis to the simultaneous
association-wide evangelistic program.

"That each state plan and promote a state-wide con-
ference on evangelism.

"That, due to constant expansion of many of our
industrial communities, mission stations and new
churches, wherever it seems advisable, be organized,
looking toward the formation of an independent
church.

"That we, the committee, urge and call upon every
Southern Baptist to believe that the prosecution of this
program will give us a unified program of evangelism
that will increase our evangelistic results many times."

III. USE OF CHURCH ORGANIZATIONS EMPHASIZED

It is noted that in the recommendation of the Southern Baptist Convention emphasis is given to the use
of church organizations in evangelism. Why not?
Through the providences of God, Southern Baptist
churches have created organizations within the church
for which there was a distinct need in soul-winning,
Bible teaching, stewardship, missions, and everything
else that touches the kingdom enterprise. These organizations are the hands and the feet of the church, the
body of Christ. Through them a church member finds
an outlet for service in every phase of work that a
New Testament Christian is supposed to do. Each organization has its courses of training that instruct the
individual in the line of service in which his organization is supposed to function. Christians are engaged
in a continuous and terrible warfare. A physical warfare where the wrestling is against flesh and blood is

symbolic of the wrestling going on in the spiritual world. The nations of the earth have branches in their armed forces—army, navy, and air corps. Recruits are trained in specific lines that are in accord with the type of action in which their branch of service will engage.

The same is true of the organizations of the church. Recruits are trained in specific lines that are in accord with the type of service in which their organization will engage. Any type of evangelism that omits using these church organizations has not only robbed itself of the help that specifically trained Christians can give, but it denies these organizations the opportunity to serve in the purpose for which they were created. Still more serious is the fact that it retards the development of the church as a unit and robs it of its efficiency in its warfare against Satan.

IV. USE THE SUNDAY SCHOOL THE FIRST WEEK

Chief of any Southern Baptist church organization in soul-winning is the Sunday school. This is true whether it be a church revival or perennial evangelism carried on from week to week. For this reason it is recommended that the Sunday school organization be used almost exclusively the first week of the revival.

1. *High Attendance Day in Sunday School*

The main problem in a revival is to get the lost and the unattached Baptists to attend the preaching services. One of the most effective methods in meeting this perplexing problem is High Attendance Day in Sunday school. In fact, God has so marvelously blessed this special method that nearly half of the conversions and additions to the churches in revivals in the Southern Baptist Convention take place in this special service. How is this done?

(1) *Set attendance objective.*—The pastor and the Sunday school superintendent should agree on an attendance objective for the Sunday school for the middle Sunday of the revival. This objective should be to break all records. Baptists will respond to a challenge. Records are being broken now in every field of human endeavor. Why not break some records for Christ in our churches? Since using High Attendance Day, the author has seen churches in cities, towns, and rural sections consistently break Sunday school attendance records of from five to a hundred years' standing. If the highest attendance record in the history of the Sunday school is 130, set the goal at 131. If it is 2,545, set the attendance goal at 2,546. Undertake to beat, by at least one, any mark that was ever made. After a tentative attendance goal is set, have a meeting with the department superintendents and obtain their consent and co-operation in the effort. This should be done at least a week before the revival begins.

Preceding the evening service of Monday after the first Sunday of the revival, have a meeting of all teachers, officers, and class officers of the Sunday school. Serve a dinner for the occasion. Break the attendance goal down by departments. Then allow time before the preaching service for a meeting by departments of at least twenty minutes, in which each department will break down the attendance goal by classes.

(2) *Plan to contact every pupil.*—In this presession meeting make plans to contact by Saturday night of that week every person enrolled in the Sunday school. The chain method may be used for making these contacts. The Baptist Book Store in each area has in stock chain links made of gummed paper (No. E-3, 500 for 80c, 1000 for $1.50). Be sure to have them on hand at this meeting. Order at least twice as many links as you

have persons enrolled in the Sunday school. The slogan is: "Don't break the chain. Do not be a missing link." Have every person in the Sunday school, from the pastor to the youngest baby in the nursery, sign a link. Of course, where children are too young to sign their names, the parents will sign for them.

(3) *Display goals and results.*—Have a placard made for each department, showing the name of the department and the attendance goal for it. Hang these placards on the wall of the church or in the church foyer where the people can see them. Have the links turned in to the superintendents each evening. Tabulate them and form a chain with the links, fastening them to the department placard to which they belong. The plan is to have signed by Saturday night the number of links that will equal the total attendance objective. When this is done, make a complete chain of all department links and stretch the chain around the walls of the church. The fact that each link represents a life makes this chain the most interesting and attractive object one can imagine.

The signing of these links puts people to work. A record number of visits will be made and interest in the revival engendered. The chain method can be used over and over in the same church without losing its effectiveness. Of course, there are many other methods that can be used in visitation. The idea is to reach the goal.

(4) *What to do with the people.*—What to do with this throng of people on Sunday morning is a far greater responsibility than the making of contacts. God has blessed the following program again and again with astounding results.

a. Meet, as usual, by departments.—Start at the usual time on Sunday morning. Plan opening assemblies that are evangelistic and conducive to soul-winning. Register all pupils. Be sure to obtain addresses of visitors, for they largely constitute the prospects for church membership.

b. Assemble by departments in the auditorium.— At 10:05 have the Sunday school, from Juniors up, march by departments into the church auditorium. Have each department seated in a special reserved section with Juniors at the front. Have organ or piano music played while they are marching. Do not make lengthy announcements. Have one song, such as "Revive Us Again" or "Jesus, Keep Me Near the Cross." The pastor should introduce the evangelist, whose message will take the place of the teaching of the lesson. The message should be brief and the way of salvation be made as plain, as simple, and as powerful as the evangelist is capable of making it, with God's help.

Follow this with an invitation that will last as long as the Holy Spirit impresses. In some churches it is well to continue until noon, having only the one service. In other cases, it is best to close the service in time for the regular morning preaching service. Adequate programs should be prepared for the Primary department on down during the period of this evangelistic service. If there has been much fervent praying and the church is spiritually ready, this will be the greatest service that many in the church have ever witnessed.

(5) *The invitation is important.*—The success of this service depends largely upon the evangelist's ability to give an invitation. Because of this, instructions are given on the subject of pressing the invitation.

"Knowing therefore the terror of the Lord, we persuade men" (2 Cor. 5: 11). The term "drawing the net" is applied to the invitation of the minister to the unchurched, the back-slidden Christians, and the un-

saved at the close of his sermon. No preacher can estimate the tremendous importance of net-drawing until
he positionizes himself on such an occasion. He must
be fully aware of the fact that he is standing in the
breach between a lost soul and an endless hell. He
must know that human agency is the instrument upon
which God depends to make the appeal to a spiritually-
blind and helpless sinner. He must realize that, if he
fails to do this, the failure may be the cause of a soul's
spending eternity in a burning hell.

That is why the apostle Paul wrote these words,
"Knowing therefore the terror of the Lord, we persuade men." That is why Paul was probably the greatest persuader of men that this world has ever known.
He said, "I could wish that myself were accursed from
Christ for my brethren, my kinsmen according to the
flesh" (Rom. 9: 3). "Therefore watch, and remember,
that by the space of three years I ceased not to warn
every one night and day with tears" (Acts 20: 31). Who
has pleaded with sinners like that? It is easy to tell people about Jesus. It is not difficult to preach Jesus. What
Christian is there who could not tell people about
Jesus, the only hope of humanity? But it is extremely
difficult to get lost people to accept Jesus as Saviour.
The matter of drawing the net is probably the chief
difference between a successful and an unsuccessful
evangelist. Therefore, the greatest, the most earnest
thought and study humanly possible on the matter of
net-drawing should be made by every preacher of the
Word of God. These suggestions about net-drawing
are addressed especially to the evangelist.

  a. Drawing the net involves power.—Drawing the
net involves every power and every gift known to the
Christian. Every faculty of our being should be at
the disposal of the Holy Spirit.

(a) *Use the power of persuasion.*—In an invitation the effort is made to persuade people to do right, not to do wrong. They are being persuaded to break with the devil and come to God. They are being persuaded to spend life on earth on the side of God instead of on the side of the devil. They are being persuaded to spend eternity in heaven instead of in hell. Convictions and hearts' concern will determine the earnestness of the speaker.

(b) *Use the power of psychology.*—Always begin with the easiest appeal and the kind of appeal that is least likely to be offensive to the hearers. Know what song the singer is going to use and do not have a hitch between the words of appeal and the beginning of the singing. As the audience rises to stand, have the music going. The appeal should be made clear to the unaffiliated to come by letter, on the promise of a letter, or by statement, and to the sinner to come forward and confess Christ as Saviour. If the response is good, stay with it. Make no different appeal until the response has stopped.

By all means, do not let the invitation drag. At every indication of lagging, change the appeal. When as many as can have been reaped by this method, ask for the easiest demonstration possible. Here it is: "All of you who are within the sound of my voice, who know Christ as your Saviour and are so grateful for God's having saved you that you are a member of the church where you live and are serving him, I want you to testify for him. We do not have time for each of you to speak words, so we shall ask you by raising your hands to testify that you are saved and are an active member of the church." When this is done, make a brief appeal to those who could not conscientiously raise their hands to put their trust in Christ. Start the music again. When this response is stopped, turn to another power of persuasion.

(c) *Use your personal workers, or the power of organization.*—Remember that the preacher is only one person. Out in the congregation may be scores of people whose hearts are on fire for the lost. Many of them are friends and relatives of the unchurched. Because of these relationships, maybe they have more influence than the preacher has with some who have not responded. Have them in mind in every maneuver you make.

(d) *Use the power of example.*—We have heard that one example is worth a thousand arguments. You must bring to the attention of the Christians, without directly telling them so, that they are to win others. For instance, here comes a teacher leading a pupil to the front to accept Christ. Stop the music long enough to say: "Isn't it a glorious thing to see a Sunday school teacher who loves God and who loves the souls of lost people lead his pupil to Christ?" That example makes other teachers start working. Maybe a boy will come forward leading his classmate to Christ. Call that to the attention of the congregation, and other pupils will begin witnessing.

Then, suppose a little girl has come forward and has made a clear-cut confession of Christ. Place her before the congregation and say something like this: "Here is a little girl only nine years of age. Her little heart was touched by the love of Jesus. She came forward. I asked, 'How old are you?' 'Nine,' she answered. 'What is it, darling, that you want to do?' 'I am trusting Jesus as my Saviour,' was her answer. That is what Jesus wanted her to do for he said, 'Suffer little children, and forbid them not, to come unto me: for of such is the kingdom of heaven.' If God's way of salvation is so

simple that a little child can understand, surely you
who are grown and mature would not offer excuses.
'And a little child shall lead them.'" Then start the
music again.

(e) *Use the power of suggestion.*—Remember that
the forces of hell are against a person who is rescuing
souls. If there is anything Satan can do effectively in
the hour of decision on life or death, it is to confuse
people and keep them from thinking. Resort then to
the power of suggestion. Stop the music and say, "Isn't
it wonderful to see a mother bring her daughter to
Christ or a father bring his son to Christ? That is a
parent's highest privilege on earth. Isn't it great to see
a deacon walk the aisle with his friend, or a brother
with a brother, a sister with a sister, a friend with a
neighbor? That, my friends, is your privilege now as
we shall sing the next number." You will be surprised
at the number of people who will wake up to the fact
that they should do something and start trying to win
others simply because you have made a suggestion.

b. Seasoning the green wood.—Now, suppose that
all who will respond have been reached. The seasoned
wood has responded to the revival fires. There will
doubtless be numbers of lost and unchurched present
who have not attended the revival before, and if they
are not saved, they may never attend another religious
service. Have your congregation seated. Now comes
the process of seasoning the green wood for the fire.
Have everyone bow in prayer. Be careful who leads
the prayer. It is safest for the evangelist to lead it. He
should cast himself wholly on the mercy of God. Remember, the evangelist can only persuade; God must
do the rest. After the prayer, make another brief appeal. Use Scripture promises that will break down
excuses like, "Behold, now is the accepted time; be-

hold, now is the day of salvation" (2 Cor. 6: 2). Sound the warnings of God like, "Boast not thyself of tomorrow; for thou knowest not what a day may bring forth" (Prov. 27: 1).

The devil is the father of excuses, and no excuse is acceptable with God. To help the personal workers identify the unchurched, once more ask that all who are saved and members of the church where they live stand and the rest remain seated. Then, once more make the appeal of your life. Call on God to help you. Call to their attention the fact that no man serves two masters, that we are either for Christ or against him. Remember, you are matching wits with the one who deceives the whole world. Have all to stand, and start the music again. Give illustrations of how you have seen personal workers bring others to Jesus. Keep singing and appealing until you have gleaned all you can.

c. *The closing appeal.*—Turn everything over to God in your own soul and seek the Holy Spirit's help. Tell those who have not responded that they are not saying no to the preacher or to the personal worker, but to God. Remind them that Jesus said, "No man can come to me, except the Father which hath sent me draw him: and I will raise him up at the last day" (John 6: 44). Tell them that you are leaving the matter entirely with them and God, that if they have had an impression or an impulse to do God's will, then God has spoken to them. Such an impression is the voice of the Spirit of God. Tell them that you will have one more stanza sung, and if no one responds, you will take it for granted that God wants the service to close. If one responds, sing another stanza and make the same proposition again. Sometimes the revival will break anew and numbers will make decisions.

(6) *Obtaining results from this service.*—The results of this evangelistic service are dependent upon three things: work, preaching, and prayer. Work will get the people there. Preaching will be effective provided adequate spiritual preparation has been made. A chain of prayer should be conducted all day Saturday, beginning at 7:00 A.M. and continuing until time for the evening service. Department superintendents and their teachers should meet for prayer each evening before the preaching service begins. Pray without ceasing. Pray until the Holy Spirit's power will be in such evidence that, as lost people gather in the service Sunday morning, they will be convicted of their sins. Pray while the evangelist preaches. Pray for the teachers and officers, for the cold and indifferent church members, and, above all, for the lost. Have faith in God and trust him for results. Lost people will attend this service in great numbers. If they are not won to Christ here, they may never be reached for him.

Outline for Teacher

I. EVERY REVIVAL SHOULD LAST TWO WEEKS

II. THE SOUTHERN BAPTIST PROGRAM OF EVANGELISM

III. USE OF CHURCH ORGANIZATIONS EMPHASIZED

IV. USE THE SUNDAY SCHOOL THE FIRST WEEK

    1. High Attendance Day in Sunday School
       (1) Set attendance objective
       (2) Plan to contact every pupil
       (3) Display goals and results
       (4) What to do with the people
       (5) The invitation is important
       (6) Obtaining results from this service

Questions for Thought and Discussion

1. Tell of the origin of the Southern Baptist program of evangelism.
2. Tell how to promote High Attendance Day in the Sunday school.

7

Using the Organizations the Second Week of the Revival

THERE are many perplexing problems in present day evangelism that tend to discourage pastors and churches. Chief of these is the poor attendance in the weekday services. This problem has caused many churches to limit the revival effort to one week instead of two. Unless this problem is solved, revival effort may finally be limited to a visitation program and Sunday services only, as some of the major denominations have done in the past, to their sorrow. This is only a step toward spiritual deterioration and tragic surrender to the world, the flesh, and the devil.

There is no doubt that churches can be maintained as such without mass evangelism. They may have a large Sunday morning attendance; they may have accessions and be large giving churches. Such was the church at Laodicea, but read what the Bible says about this church.

"And unto the angel of the church of the Laodiceans write; These things saith the Amen, the faithful and true witness, the beginning of the creation of God; I know thy works, that thou art neither cold nor hot: I would thou wert cold or hot. So then because thou art lukewarm, and neither cold nor hot, I will spue thee out of my mouth. Because thou sayest, I am rich, and increased with goods, and have need of nothing;

and knowest not that thou art wretched, and miserable, and poor, and blind, and naked: I counsel thee to buy of me gold tried in the fire, that thou mayest be rich; and white raiment, that thou mayest be clothed, and that the shame of thy nakedness do not appear; and anoint thine eyes with eyesalve, that thou mayest see. As many as I love, I rebuke and chasten: be zealous therefore, and repent" (Rev. 3: 14-19).

There is no substitute for preaching the gospel, and there is no substitute for mass evangelism. To abandon mass evangelism just because it is difficult is no more excusable on the part of a pastor and church than to abandon the doctrine of repentance because it is difficult to get people to repent. God expects us to find a way to meet these problems and solve them with his help. God wants to revive his churches. He is willing to send a revival upon his people if we are willing to seek his methods for the day in which we live and then pay the price of carrying them out.

I. STIMULATE ATTENDANCE THROUGH THE CHURCH ORGANIZATIONS

It is the author's belief that anything that needs to be done can be done with the understanding that it is in harmony with the will of God. It certainly is God's will for his churches to be revived. They are all that he has in this world. They are to carry out the program that Jesus assigned to them before his ascension. Spiritually cold and passionless churches cannot fulfil Christ's purpose for them. If attendance on the part of saint and sinner is the chief problem in a church revival, the hands and hearts must be set to solve it.

The second week of a church revival should be harvest week. During the first week the foundation for an ingathering has been laid through preaching, praying, singing, and visiting. As a rule, it now takes one week to interest and revive the church members. The second week should be used to reach the lost for Christ and to reclaim the unaffiliated Baptists. This can be done by careful and prayerful planning on the part of the pastor, the evangelist, and the church organizations for special nights.

These special services are now discussed. It is optional, of course, with the church as to which ones to have and when to have them. There are three distinct classes of churches—city, town, and rural. These special features will be handled differently because of the lack of facilities in many of the smaller churches. The purpose of these suggestions is to advance an idea. The church can carry the idea out in its own way, governed of course by local conditions.

1. *Men's Night*

Men's Night is sponsored by the Brotherhood of the church. It may be held on Monday. In case the church has no such organization, then use the adult men's classes, headed by the Sunday school superintendent. The success of Men's Night depends on careful planning, hard work, and much prayer. Two weeks before the revival begins, the pastor and the officers of the Brotherhood should meet and make thorough plans for the service. Bear in mind always that this night is to have more than a big attendance as its objective. It is to reach lost men for Christ.

(1) *How to proceed.*—Plan to have supper for those who attend. Have plenty of names of prospects to be invited to the supper. Agree on the price of the tickets (if admittance is by ticket) and how the ticket should read. Tickets can be printed or mimeographed. The

men who are members of the church should pay for their own tickets, but all visitors are to be admitted free. The expense for meals served visitors should be paid for either by the men who invite them or out of the treasury of the Brotherhood. Regardless of the financial arrangement, do not charge the visitor for his meal.

(2) *A suggested program.*—Here is a suggested program:

6:30 P.M.: Supper served, preceded by singing of doxology and prayer

7:00 P.M.: Group singing—three familiar hymns

7:10 P.M.: Members of church will introduce their guests

7:20 P.M.: Special music

7:30 P.M.: Remarks by the pastor, who introduces the evangelist. Pastor invites all to remain for the preaching service. On this occasion have the choir loft filled with men. Have special music by a male quartet, if one is available. On a number of occasions the author has seen men won to Christ at this service. The pastor should give special recognition to the Brotherhood and to the men who are present. Special message and appeal should be made by the evangelist for the unsaved to accept Christ and for unaffiliated Baptists to unite with the church.

2. *Women's Night*

Women's Night is sponsored by the Woman's Missionary Society. This service, too, should be planned two weeks in advance. Have a meeting of the pastor with officers of the W.M.S. Arrange for the church roll to be up to date and names of women of the church to be placed on cards (ten names to each card) with addresses and telephone numbers. Then have a supply of

cards with the names of prospects. Have at least one
prospect for each member of the W.M.S. to contact.
On the day before the revival have in the hand of each
member of the W.M.S. a card with ten names of members and one prospect to be contacted by phone, visit,
or otherwise, and invited to the service. Fill the choir
loft with women at this service, and have special music
by women. The pastor should give special recognition
to the W.M.S. and to the women present. This presents
a rare opportunity for the evangelist to urge the unsaved to accept Christ and the unaffiliated Baptists to
unite with the church.

3. *Sunday School Night*

Sunday School Night may be on Wednesday. This
service should afford a wonderful opportunity to reach
those unchurched that were not reached for Christ and
the church the middle Sunday of the revival. This service, too, should be well planned, as follows: The pastor
should make a strong announcement of this service on
the previous Sunday morning. Then have a special
meeting of all teachers and officers before or after the
preaching service the Monday night before. Here lay
plans as follows:

Teachers contact all members of class by visit,
phone, or letter and urge that they be present Sunday
School Night.

Assemble by departments (or classes if not depart-
mentized) thirty minutes before the preaching service
—by departments and then by classes just as on Sunday
morning. Teachers lead in prayer for the unsaved who
are enrolled in Sunday school, for unsaved loved ones,
and for the service to follow.

March into the auditorium by classes. The pastor
should give special recognition to each department.

The message by the evangelist should be one of simplicity on the way of salvation. This service affords an ideal opportunity for personal work during the invitation, provided it has been duly preceded by prayer.

4. Training Union Night

On Thursday have Training Union Night. On the middle Sunday evening, preceding Training Union hour, the pastor, Training Union director, and officers of the Training Union should meet in a body and lay plans that will challenge this organization to do something special on Training Union Night.

Plan not only for all Training Union members to be contacted and present, but to reach out and invite everybody to attend Training Union Night at the revival. Give out cards with names of prospects. Have young people to pledge to invite ten other young people to the service, set attendance goals by unions and by departments, work for enthusiasm, and God will reward with a visitation of his power.

Plan for special music, quartets, duets, and other special numbers.

Give everyone something to do. Have young people as ushers; and have young ladies to pin ribbons, on which are given the attendance goals for the closing service of Training Union Sunday night, on the lapels of coats and dresses of the people as they enter the church. This can be a lively, inspiring service if adequate plans are made.

5. Family Night

Set Family Night for Friday. God in his infinite wisdom has divided civilization into units, namely, the home and the nation. The home is the oldest and the smallest. It is likewise the most important. Nationali-

ties are the curse of the human race. They were
brought into existence because of sin, in the building
of the tower of Babel, Genesis 11: 1-9. Most of the wars
throughout all history have stemmed from the curse
of nationalities. But the home is the nerve center of
civilization. The strength of the government lies in the
homes of the nation. When homes become corrupt and
defiled, all society is affected, for society is made up of
homes. A church is no more religious than the homes
which constitute its membership. People cannot live
like angels on Sunday and like the devil the other six
days of the week. The devil knows all this too well, and
today he is striking with all of his fury at the homes of
this world, and especially the homes of America. There
is no getting around the fact that many American
homes are on the rocks morally and spiritually. Surely
every church revival should observe Family Night for
the sake of its homes. Children will not be in school on
Saturday, and they can all attend services on Friday
night.

What can be accomplished on Family Night? Family
Night in a revival can be the breaking point for God in
the meeting. It will meet the needs of the people. It
will touch their lives where they live daily. It will
rightly interpret the Christian message on marriage
and homemaking. It will point out the responsibilities
of father, mother, husband, wife, and children—so-
cially, economically, and spiritually. The home is the
storehouse of affection. With the home go more sacred
memories than in all other human relations combined,
ten times over. The nearest thing to heaven on this
earth is a happy Christian home. The nearest thing to
hell on this earth is an unhappy, broken home. Does
not the home deserve emphasis in our churches and in
our revivals?

Here are some suggestions as to the success of Family Night:

Publicize it vigorously before the meeting begins and at three services beforehand. The evangelist should prepare his best sermon and at least plan the best program of music. Precede the night of its observance with letters, postcards, phone calls, and visits. Announce that recognition will be given to the largest family present and to the couple that has been married the longest. When large families are to be recognized, begin like this: "All families represented by only one person tonight, please stand." Then "all families represented by only two persons, please stand," and so on until the largest family present has stood. Thus, recognition has been given to everyone present. Announce that gifts will be made to the various groups: A Bible to the largest family and a subscription to *Home Life* or some good religious book for the home to others. Have these all prepared and ready ahead of time. Have Family Altar Commitment Cards ready for those who will pledge to have family worship. (No. FA 1. Price $2.00 for 100. Order these from the Baptist Book Store serving your area.)

Have families sit together in the service. The choir members may leave their places and sit with their families. The pastor should sit with his family, provided a guest preacher is doing the preaching. This is home night, family night, and God's night.

6. *Prospect Night*

As far as fruitage is concerned, Prospect Night is the best service in a two weeks' revival, with the possible exception of the combined service on the middle Sunday. Southern Baptist churches are just beginning to realize the potentialities of Prospect Night. From one to fifty additions to the churches are being recorded now on Prospect Night in multitudes of revivals. So successful was this special night in one simultaneous crusade that all records as to additions to the churches were broken. Prospect Night was first initiated for men only. Someone discovered that the unchurched men who came were separated from their families. For this reason they hesitated to make decisions, desiring, of course, that others of the family make decisions for church membership with them. Then the idea prevailed that many unsaved women and children could be reached along with the men. So Prospect Night came to include men, women, and children. Here is a suggested plan and program for the occasion:

The date should be Thursday night of the last week of the revival.

The plans for it should be made on Monday night of the last week of the revival, and not later than Tuesday night. The planning committee should be composed of pastor, officers and teachers of the Sunday school, officers of the Training Union, the Woman's Missionary Union, the Brotherhood, and the deacons. In fact, this is a church affair.

Tickets like this should be printed and ready:

ADMIT ONE
to
PROSPECT NIGHT DINNER

First Baptist Church
November 1, _____
6:30 P.M.

A good meal should be planned for the occasion and paid for by the church, without cost to anyone who attends. To sell tickets or to charge for the meal will defeat its purpose and will hinder the soul-winning effort. The church member's ticket is a prospect. The tickets are for the guests or prospects only. A prospect is an unaffiliated Baptist or an unsaved person. The Sunday school roll should be combed for prospects. The names of unchurched people obtained through the religious census and otherwise should be ready for distribution at the meeting planning for Prospect Night.

Announcements clear and in detail should be made from the pulpit, and tickets should be given to those who desire them at the morning and evening services. Every church member, regardless of age, should try to find a prospect and invite him to the supper. There are scriptural grounds for such an effort (Luke 14: 16-24).

The deadline for reservations should be 10:00 A.M. of the day on which the service is to be held.

A suggested program is as follows:

6:30 P.M.: Supper served

7:00 P.M.: Pastor presides. Have song service of familiar gospel songs

7:10 P.M.: Pastor has church members introduce their guests

7:20 P.M.: Special music

7:25 P.M.: Pastor gives brief history of the church, referring principally to facilities for Sunday school, Training Union, and plans for the future. He should stress the value of churches in the community and the need of a church home for all. Then he introduces the evangelist, invites all to stay for the preaching service, and has the evangelist close with a prayer.

The evangelist should have in mind as he preaches and in his appeal that this is the greatest opportunity he will likely have to persuade the lost to accept Christ as Saviour and to appeal to nonresident members to affiliate with the church. He should always bear in mind the words of Paul, "Knowing therefore the terror of the Lord, we persuade men" (2 Cor. 5: 11).

II. BAPTIZING CONVERTS IN A REVIVAL.

The ordinance of baptism belongs to the church.

1. *The Importance of Baptism*

In Christ's commission, baptism is given second place only to regeneration. Teaching the new convert "to observe all things whatsoever I have commanded you" has to follow baptism for the simple reason that such a thing cannot be done until a person is baptized. So vital is the meaning of baptism and so necessary is baptism in its observance that not only did Jesus himself set the example in his act of obedience, but heaven was moved as John the Baptist buried Christ in the waters of Jordan. So overwhelming was this divine act that the Third Person of the Trinity emerged from the portals of the heavens above, clothed himself in the form of a dove, God's emblem of peace, and alighted on the dripping garments of the Son of God. So far-reaching is the meaning of baptism and it so rejoices the heart of the Father when observed by his children that he could not contain his joy when his only begotten Son had set the example for all of the redeemed to follow, by exclaiming from his throne on high to the earth beneath, "This is my beloved Son, in whom I am well pleased" (Matt. 17: 5). Before Jesus stepped into the water, he gave his evaluation of baptism with these words, "For thus it becometh us to fulfil all righteousness" (Matt. 3: 15).

Simon Peter emphatically stated to convicted sinners at Pentecost, "Repent, and be baptized every one of you in the name of Jesus Christ for the remission of sins" (Acts 2: 38). He thus implied that when one has repented he will reveal the fact by following his Lord in baptism. In order that no one need imply that baptism is essential to salvation or that it contains any element of saving efficacy, Peter gives a commentary on its meaning, "The like figure whereunto even baptism doth also now save us (not the putting away of the filth of the flesh, but the answer of a good conscience toward God) by the resurrection of Jesus Christ" (1 Peter 3: 21). Water has nothing to do with removing "the filth of the flesh." That is done by the blood of the Lamb. "But if we walk in the light, as he is in the light, we have fellowship one with another, and the blood of Jesus Christ his Son cleanseth us from all sin" (1 John 1: 7). Peter leaves no doubt about the effect baptism has on the conscience of God's children in his statement, "But the answer of a good conscience toward God."

2. *The Christian Attitude Toward Baptism*

In the face of these mighty truths one can see God's purpose in evangelism through his churches. If God himself places such value on baptism and heaven so rejoices when it is observed, what should be the attitude of Christians toward it? That is one great reason for church-centered evangelism. It is displeasing to God to lead the unsaved to Christ and leave them there. The author's suggestion is this: During a church revival, where facilities for baptizing converts are accessible, the ordinance should be observed every night, even if only one person is prepared for it. If the ordinance is properly observed with all of its sacred beauty, it stimulates the revival as nothing else can. The last Sunday of the revival should close with a baptismal service. In the rural churches where converts are baptized in the open, there should be "dinner on the ground" and the countryside urged to come for the baptismal service. Make much of this service in a way that it will glorify Christ and carry out the true meaning of baptism. Of course, blessed is the church that is adorned with a beautiful baptistry such as will add to the beauty of the occasion.

III. AN EARNEST REMINDER

The author has endeavored to give in this and preceding chapters plans and methods for reaching high attendance goals in a church revival. These are only a few of many plans and methods that are being used effectively by pastors and evangelists in the work of evangelism throughout our land. But there is one earnest reminder which should be called to the attention of all who read this book: All of the best plans and methods known to the Christian world will not save a lost soul. God uses methods to reach the sinful heart of man, but they are as brass without his power. If Christians are willing to humble themselves and pray, the power of God will be in evidence. Always remember, "This is the word of the Lord unto Zerubbabel, saying, Not by might, nor by power, but by my spirit, saith the Lord of hosts" (Zech. 4: 6). There is no situation pertaining to a revival in any Baptist church so difficult that victory cannot be obtained through prayer and work.

Outline for Teacher

I. STIMULATE ATTENDANCE THROUGH THE CHURCH ORGANIZATIONS
   1. Men's Night
      (1) How to proceed
      (2) A suggested program
   2. Women's Night
   3. Sunday School Night
   4. Training Union Night
   5. Family Night
   6. Prospect Night

II. BAPTIZING CONVERTS IN A REVIVAL
   1. The Importance of Baptism
   2. The Christian Attitude Toward Baptism

III. AN EARNEST REMINDER

Questions for Thought and Discussion

1. Which of the special night attendance stimulators do you think will work best in your church?
2. How can the ordinance of baptism be most effectively used to promote soul-winning in the revival?

8

Conserving the Results of Evangelism

THE most justifiable criticism that can be made of all that Southern Baptists are doing today is their failure to conserve the results of their evangelistic efforts.

I. SOME SHOCKING FACTS

Here are some shocking facts from the 1954 *Southern Baptist Handbook.*

1. *Nonresident Members*

At the end of 1953 there were 2,460,437 nonresident church members, leaving a total resident membership of 5,425,579. Of the total resident membership of 5,425,579, at least 25 per cent are completely inactive. By inactive is meant that they do not attend church except on rare occasions, they do not contribute to the church's financial program, they are not enrolled in Sunday school or in any other church organization, and they do not bear witness for Christ. If this estimate is correct (it is believed to be conservative), there are 1,356,395 resident members who are inactive and just as much lost to Christ and his church as if they were nonresident members. The nonresident members plus the inactive resident members total 3,816,832. The total church membership as reported in the 1954 *Southern Baptist Handbook* is 7,886,016. This would mean that 48.4 per cent of the entire membership of Southern Baptist churches is lost to the cause of Christ.

Here is the ratio of baptisms to church membership reported by states in the 1954 *Southern Baptist Handbook:*

Oregon-Washington	1 to 7.6
California	1 to 8.7
Kansas	1 to 9.3
Arizona	1 to 9.5
New Mexico	1 to 13.8
Florida	1 to 17
Maryland	1 to 18.6
Illinois	1 to 19
Oklahoma	1 to 19
Arkansas	1 to 19.8
Missouri	1 to 20.5
District of Columbia	1 to 21.1
Texas	1 to 21.1
Tennessee	1 to 22.3
Alabama	1 to 23.2
Louisiana	1 to 24.1
Kentucky	1 to 24.4
North Carolina	1 to 24.4
Georgia	1 to 24.7
South Carolina	1 to 24.8
Mississippi	1 to 25.4
Virginia	1 to 25.9

2. *What Real Enlistment Would Mean*

The aforementioned statistics on baptisms look very bad, and they are bad. But they do not rightly represent Southern Baptists' efforts in evangelism for the simple reason that 48.4 per cent of members reported are contributing absolutely nothing toward winning lost people to Christ and to his church. If this 48.4 per cent were enlisted as the other 51.6 per cent are, the figure would read like this:

Oregon-Washington . . . . 1 to 4
California . . . . 1 to 4.5
Kansas . . . . 1 to 4.8
Arizona . . . . 1 to 4.9
New Mexico . . . . 1 to 7.1
Florida . . . . 1 to 8.8
Maryland . . . . 1 to 9.6
Illinois . . . . 1 to 9.8
Oklahoma . . . . 1 to 9.8
Arkansas . . . . 1 to 10.2
Missouri . . . . 1 to 10.6
District of Columbia . . . . . 1 to 10.9
Texas . . . . 1 to 10.9
Tennessee . . . . 1 to 11.5
Alabama . . . . 1 to 12
Louisiana . . . . 1 to 12.4
Kentucky . . . . 1 to 12.6
North Carolina . . . . 1 to 12.6
Georgia . . . . 1 to 12.7
South Carolina . . . . 1 to 12.8
Mississippi . . . . 1 to 13.1
Virginia . . . . 1 to 13.4

Had the 48.4 per cent of unenlisted members been enlisted as the 51.6 per cent were, the ratio of baptisms for Southern Baptists in 1953 would have been 1 to 11.2 instead of 1 to 21.8, and total baptisms would have been 701,216 instead of 361,835. What is true in the field of evangelism would be true in stewardship—money for local church work and for the Cooperative Program. What is true in the field of evangelism would be true in enrolments of the Sunday school, the Training Union, Woman's Missionary Union, and the Brotherhood. Therefore, conservation of evangelistic results is the responsibility of every pastor, every church, every organization in a church, and every agency of the Southern Baptist Convention. Its necessity is so critical and so alarming that it should stir everyone who has the interest of the cause of Christ and concern for souls to do something about it. Not only is the cause of Christ involved in conservation of evangelistic results, but the happiness and the welfare of these 3,816,832 unenlisted people and their families are involved.

3. WHAT IS THE REMEDY?

To find a remedy for the problem of unenlisted church members is a must for Southern Baptists. It is too serious a matter to neglect or to ignore. It is something for which God will hold us accountable at the judgment. To offer an adequate program of conservation of evangelistic results is too much to expect of any one person. However, here are some observations.

(1) *The problem of conservation is not caused by the reception of unsaved people into the churches.*— No Southern Baptist church would knowingly approve an unregenerate person for baptism or receive such a one into church membership. Of course, there are bound to be some who get into our churches without salvation, but they are few.

(2) *One of the reasons for failure in conservation is the reception of new members into spiritually cold churches.*—Should there be an ingathering of souls into a church that has not been revived, the babes in Christ will be treated as stepchildren. As an illustration: Have you prayed and agonized for some particular unsaved person, God heard your prayers, and that individual was saved? You felt that you were instrumental in his coming to Christ as Saviour. Have you not had a deeper personal interest in that person's spiritual growth than you have in the spiritual growth of another in whose salvation you had no part? What is true

of you is true of a church. The author once witnessed
the conversion of a man for whom the church had
prayed over twenty-five years. Hundreds of people had
prayed scores of times that this man might be saved.
The night he made his public profession of faith in
Christ the people were overjoyed. Everyone rejoiced,
and it seemed that every person tried to make the new
convert know that he loved him. He was the object of
special interest every time he entered the church door.
The Sunday school teacher went out of his way to
recognize him and to help in every way he could spiritually. Three years from the day of this man's conversion he died. The author conducted his funeral. It
seemed that everyone in the church who knew him and
was not providentially hindered attended the funeral.
Why? Because they had made a definite contribution
to his salvation, and from it there was created an unusual affection in their hearts for him.

(3) *The right type of preaching is imperative.*—The
evangelist should do the kind of preaching that makes
much of the Word of God. He must deal faithfully and
honestly with sin and God's only way of salvation. He
is not to have as his objective simply to get decisions,
but to get people genuinely converted and added to
the church. "Then they that gladly received his word
were baptized: and the same day there were added
unto them about three thousand souls" (Acts 2: 41).
"Praising God, and having favour with all the people.
And the Lord added to the church daily such as should
be saved" (Acts 2: 47).

That is why the author is not in favor of "union"
meetings. Preaching that is constructive must go further than the new birth. The most vital transaction
known to man is the salvation of the soul. Close to it
and almost equal in its importance is the salvation of a

life. This should be pointed out to the congregation by the evangelist with all the vigor he possesses. Subjects like baptism, the New Testament church, stewardship of life, talents, and property, the meaning of church membership, and others applicable to the saved person should be included in the evangelist's sermons. Baptist preachers preaching to Baptist churches can and will do this kind of preaching. It is the responsibility of the evangelist to preach in such a way as to lay the right kind of foundation upon which the superstructure of conservation can be erected.

(4) *The new member must be properly received when he unites with the church*

a. By the pastor.—It has been the author's privilege to witness the reception of church members in churches of all sizes. It is amazing to see the variety of methods different pastors employ in presenting new members to the church for their reception. In some instances it is done so awkwardly that it becomes embarrassing to the new member and to the congregation. Others are genuine artists at presenting the applicant to the congregation. The reception of new members should be an occasion of great joy to everyone. The name of the new member should be pronounced accurately and read loudly enough for the congregation to hear. The pastor should be pleasant and should manifest a genuine joy in his own heart. He should say a brief word of welcome in a way that would please the new member and stimulate the congregation in its joy because of the occasion. The pastor should show such a personal interest in the new member that the audience will know that he has a shepherd heart.

b. By the congregation.—The congregation has distinct reason for rejoicing and for displaying interest in the reception of new members—the simple realization of what is taking place. A soul has been redeemed from sin; a life has been saved for service; Satan has been robbed of one more of his victims; a name has been written in the Lamb's book of life and no one can erase it; a soul has escaped the eternal fires of hell and, praise God, will spend eternity in heaven. That is the reason, for "I say unto you, that likewise joy shall be in heaven over one sinner that repenteth, more than over ninety and nine just persons, which need no repentance" (Luke 15: 7). If there is rejoicing in heaven over one sinner that has repented, how should members of the church act?

One of the saddest of sights when God blesses a service with new-born souls is when the congregation coldly walks out without giving expression of joy or even welcome to new-born souls or to those who come by letter to cast their lot with their brothers and sisters in Christ. Always, without fail, the hand of Christian fellowship should be extended new members by the congregation. This should be accompanied by music either by the choir or the accompanying instruments. The author shall never forget the overwhelming joy that came to his heart when he stood in line with his wife and other members and received a handclasp and a hearty welcome by hundreds of members of the church. Again and again individuals would say: "I am happy that you found the Lord. May God bless you." That reception gave to him a new and a true concept of genuine Christianity. Many churches have someone to come forward and stand by the new member on his reception and to sponsor him until he is thoroughly orientated. This is a wonderful practice.

c. The new member should be visited.—By all means the new member should be visited the week that he unites with the church. This should be done by a deacon, a man of God who understands how to deal with new members. Some churches are carrying this out with splendid results. The visitor should take along with him any materials the church has prepared for those who have just become members of the church family. A questionnaire such as is exhibited on page 110 should be filled out by the visitor. The information obtained from this questionnaire should be transferred to separate cards for use by all the church organizations. The benefits derived from the follow-up work of this visit are obvious. Great help is obtained in knowing where the new member should be in the various organizations of the church.

Everything mentioned in this chapter can be done by any church. Many are probably doing them, and more. But do not make the mistake of thinking that such things are adequate in conserving the lives of new members.

The answer to the problem of enlistment of new members will be found only in a Southern Baptist program. That is what it should be. It should be unified, and it should be revised from time to time as pastors and denominational leaders learn more about how conservation is done. It is high time for pastors and churches to take heed of the necessity for such a program. In 1953 there were 834,135 recruits added to the churches of the Southern Baptist Convention. Of this number, 361,835 came on profession of faith. Because of the great Convention-wide Simultaneous Revival Crusade in 1955, the number of recruits for enlistment should go beyond a million. This presents a permanent and distinct challenge to Southern Baptist churches. It is time that attention should be given to this tremendous responsibility.

INFORMATION SHEET FOR NEW MEMBERS

Date _____

Name _____

Residence Address _____

Residence Phone _____

Business Address _____

Business Phone _____

Born: Day _____ Month _____ Year _____

Are you enrolled in Sunday school? _____ Training Union? _____

W.M.S.? _____

Are you an ordained deacon? _____ Ordained Minister? _____

In what churches have you previously held membership? _____

What offices have you held in

1. Sunday school? _____

2. Training Union? _____

3. Woman's Missionary Union? _____

4. Brotherhood? _____

5. Vacation Bible School? _____

What church offices have you held, such as clerk, committee chairman,

usher? _____

Would you like to sing in the choir? _____

What phase of church work do you like best? _____

With what age group do you like best to work? _____

Have you made a pledge to the church budget? _____

Will you now? _____

List below other members of your family, household, or acquaintance whom you would like to see in the family of our church:

Name _____ Age _____ Address _____

Name _____ Age _____ Address _____

Name _____ Age _____ Address _____

What suggestions would you make for our church?

II. the orientation program of southern baptists

The Southern Baptist program of orientation for new members consists of the study of a book of seven chapters entitled *Your Life and Your Church* (revised edition, price 35¢), by Dr. James L. Sullivan. The subjects of these seven chapters are:

The Meaning of Your Christian Experience
The Meaning of Church Membership
You and Your Church
Your Stewardship
Your Testimony
Your Home and Your Church
Your All for Christ

This class should be counted a unit in the Training Union. On the last night, the members should be assigned to unions in the Training Union. The complete course of training in church membership in Southern Baptist churches is the Training Union.

1. *The Orientation Course Should be Sponsored by the Training Union*

The Training Union was created in 1896 to train Baptists in church membership. The unit in which the new members will meet is the "Pastor's Class," a part of the Training Union. Copies of *Your Life and Your Church* should be ordered along with other Training Union literature.

2. *The Pastor Should Teach It*

As a rule, the pastor can teach this course better than any other member of the church. His teaching all new members will help him to get better acquainted with them, and it will help the new members to know their pastor better.

No church member is thoroughly orientated into the life of his church until he is enrolled in the organizations the church has for him. But a church should not stop at orientation. It should continue to teach study course books in doctrines and methods until the individual is thoroughly capable of service for his master.

III. CONCLUSION

This book was written with a purpose. That purpose may be partially hidden because most of the context is devoted to methods and programs. Without methods and programs, convictions and zeal cannot be carried out. Many churches are in a state of tragic ineffectiveness today. It is not that they lack faithfulness to the cause of Christ. They lack power and appeal to challenge the masses to action in a period when the world stands at the crossroads—as did the Hebrew nation when on Mount Carmel Elijah cried to them out of his soul, "How long halt ye between two opinions? if the Lord be God, follow him: but if Baal, then follow him" (1 Kings 18: 21).

Baptist churches have the organizations, if only there were behind the organizations the will and the spirit on the part of the churches to use them for the purpose for which they were conceived. The situation is similar to that of a nation at war which has the weapons to conquer its enemy but has not the spirit and the determination to use them.

There is no choice for the churches in the warfare in which they are engaged. Satan cannot be appeased and churches cannot escape his fury by resorting to cowardly indifference. Neither can churches satisfy God in standing aloof from revivals and in trying to escape the responsibility and the purpose Jesus had for them by joining up with modern religious movements. Christians are only deluding themselves in depending upon religious movements for a nation-shaking revival. There will be no lasting blessing to America and to the world until churches and pastors rise up in the spirit of humility and repentance and take Christ at his word when he said, "Upon this rock I will build my church; and the gates of hell shall not prevail against it" (Matt. 16: 18). New Testament churches did this, and present-day New Testament churches will do it again.

Satan is a military strategist. He is not seriously opposed to any kind of religious program or movement, regardless of how impressive it may appear, if only he can destroy the one institution that Christ founded with which to defeat the devil and bring in the kingdom of God. It must be remembered that more than five thousand Southern Baptist churches reported no baptisms in 1953. Multitudes of churches have grown so cold and weak that the thought of trying to have a revival meets with dread and indifference, when it should be a privilege and an opportunity for rejoicing.

It is not possible for any person to write all that should be said about a church revival. This book was written with a prayer that it may stimulate a desire on the part of pastors and church members to lay hold on the promises of Christ to his churches to the end that a genuine revival may come to every church, regardless of size or location.

Outline for Teacher

   I. SOME SHOCKING FACTS

     1. Nonresident Members
     2. What Real Enlistment Would Mean
     3. What Is the Remedy?
       (1) The problem of conservation is not caused by the reception of unsaved people into the churches
       (2) One of the reasons for failure in conservation is the reception of new members into spiritually cold churches
       (3) The right type of preaching is imperative
       (4) The new member must be properly received when he unites with the church

  II. THE ORIENTATION PROGRAM OF SOUTHERN BAPTISTS

     1. The Orientation Course Should be Sponsored by the Training Union
     2. The Pastor Should Teach It

 III. CONCLUSION

Questions for Thought and Discussion

1. How many of the members of your church are inactive?
2. How may new members be conserved?
3. What results have been achieved this week through the visitation of prospects?

QUESTIONS FOR REVIEW AND EXAMINATION

FOR instructions concerning the examination and the requesting of awards, see Directions Concerning the Teaching and the Study of This Book for Credit, page 118.

CHAPTER I

1. Why is the Bible the only source of information about the origin of the church?
2. When was the first Baptist church organized?
3. How do we know that Jesus founded the church before his crucifixion?
4. Why is the time of the beginning of the church important?

CHAPTER II

5. What do evangelists see in the Bible?
6. What part does the church play in the great conflict?
7. What are the three aspects of the Great Commission?
8. What did Satan do to the seven churches of the Revelation?
9. What is necessary for a church to have a genuine revival?

CHAPTER III

10. Differentiate "evangelism" and "soul-winning."
11. What is the evangelism church council?
12. Discuss the personnel and work of the evangelism church council.
13. Why is one church revival a year not enough?
14. What is the simultaneous evangelistic crusade?

CHAPTER IV

15. What is a genuine church revival?
16. What are the essential elements in a church revival?
17. Discuss the preparation that a church must make for its revival.
18. Why is a religious census necessary?
19. Discuss the part that cottage prayer meetings should have in preparation for a revival.

CHAPTER V

20. What are the advantages of the morning service during a revival?
21. Why is gospel music the best music for a revival?
22. Discuss the qualities of the song leader for a revival.
23. What are the responsibilities of the revival choir?
24. What is the place of prayer during a revival?
25. Discuss personal work during the revival.

CHAPTER VI

26. What are the main points in the Southern Baptist program of evangelism?
27. How may the Sunday school be used to promote the revival?
28. Discuss the special service on Sunday morning of the middle Sunday of the revival.

CHAPTER VII

29. How may Men's Night be made a success?
30. Discuss the place of Family Night in stimulating revival attendance.
31. What can be done to make Prospect Night an outstanding event of the revival?

CHAPTER VIII

32. What was the real ratio of baptisms to church membership in 1953?

33. What is the remedy for the enlistment of inactive Southern Baptist church members?

34. What is the Southern Baptist program of orientation for new members?

35. What has this course meant to you?

DIRECTIONS FOR THE TEACHING AND THE STUDY OF THIS BOOK FOR CREDIT

I. DIRECTIONS FOR THE TEACHER

1. Ten class periods of forty-five minutes each, or the equivalent, are required for the completion of the book for credit.

2. The teacher of the class will be given an award if he requests it.

3. The teacher shall give a written examination covering the subject matter in the textbook, and the student shall make a minimum grade of 70 per cent. The examination may take the form of assigned work to be done between the class sessions, or as a final examination at the end of the course.

Exception: All who attend all of the class sessions, who read the book through by the close of the course, and who, in the judgment of the teacher, do the classwork satisfactorily may be exempted from taking the examination.

4. In the Graded Training Union Study Course, a seal for Course IX, Soul-winning, is granted to adults for the completion of this book.

Sunday school credit may be elected by the pupil. Applications for Sunday school awards should be sent to the state Sunday school department and for Training Union awards to the state Training Union department. These departments will provide the forms for these applications. They should be made in duplicate and both copies sent.

II. DIRECTIONS FOR THE STUDENT

1. *In Classwork*

(1) The pupil must attend at least six of the ten forty-five-minute periods to be entitled to take the class examination.

(2) The pupil must certify that the book has been read. (In rare cases where pupils may find it impracticable to read the book before the completion of the classwork, the

teacher may accept a promise to read the book carefully within the next two weeks.)

(3) The pupil must take a written examination and make a minimum grade of 70 per cent. (All who attend all of the class sessions, who read the book through by the close of the course, and who, in the judgment of the teacher, do satisfactory classwork may be exempted from taking the examination.)

2. *Individual Study by Correspondence*

Those who for any reason wish to study the book without the guidance of a teacher will use one of the following methods:

(1) Write answers to questions printed in the book, or

(2) Write a development of the chapter outlines.

In either case the student must read the book through.

Students may find profit in studying the text together, but where awards are requested, individual papers are required. Carbon copies or duplicates in any form cannot be accepted.

All written work done by such students on books for Sunday school credit should be sent to the state Sunday school secretary. All of such work done on books for Training Union credit should be sent to the state Training Union secretary.

III. INTERCHANGE OF CREDIT AND AWARDS ON COMPARABLE SUBJECTS

One award, either for Training Union or Sunday school, is granted for completing this book.

J. E. Lambdin
Secretary
Training Union Department
Baptist Sunday School Board

C. Aubrey Hearn
Director of the Study Course